CRITICAL THINKING: TABLE OF CONTENTS

Introduction 2

Curriculum Correlation 4

Letter to Parents..................................5

Assessment Test..................................6

Student Progress Chart 8

UNIT 1: Knowledge
Classifying..9
Real and Fanciful 12
Fact and Opinion..................................14
Definition and Example 16
Outlining and Summarizing 18
Unit Assessment Test 20

UNIT 2: Comprehension
Comparing and Contrasting 22
Identifying Structure 24
Steps in a Process 26
Figural Relationships...........................28
Comparing Word Meanings.................29
Identifying Main Ideas.........................31
Identifying Relationships.....................33
Unit Assessment Test 36

UNIT 3: Application
Ordering Objects 38
Estimating 41
Anticipating Probabilities 43
Inferring..45
Changes in Word Meanings 48
Unit Assessment Test 50

UNIT 4: Analysis
Judging Completeness 52
Relevance of Information.....................54
Abstract or Concrete............................56
Logic of Actions...................................57
Elements of a Selection.......................59
Story Logic 60
Recognizing Fallacies 62
Unit Assessment Test 64

UNIT 5: Synthesis
Communicating Ideas 66
Planning Projects.................................68
Building Hypotheses............................70
Drawing Conclusions 72
Proposing Alternatives........................75
Unit Assessment Test 77

UNIT 6: Evaluation
Testing Generalizations 79
Developing Criteria 81
Judging Accuracy.................................83
Making Decisions 85
Identifying Values................................88
Mood of a Story...................................91
Unit Assessment Test 93

Answer Key..95

© Steck-Vaughn Company   Critical Thinking 5, SV 6216-4

Teacher Introduction

Overview
Steck-Vaughn Critical Thinking is a program designed to teach thinking skills. The skills are organized according to Benjamin Bloom's *Taxonomy of Educational Objectives*.* These skills include some of the seven intelligences from the theory of multiple intelligences, such as linguistic, spatial, and logical-mathematical. Pupils are taught skills that have been identified as being particularly helpful in developing four stages of thinking - Knowledge, Comprehension, Application, and Analysis. At grades 3, 4, and 5 pupils move into the higher level skills of Synthesis and Evaluation.

Program Philosophy
Direct teaching of thinking skills provides pupils with the opportunity to focus on **thinking** rather than on specific content. Practicing these skills will enable students to develop strategies which will enhance their ability to do well not only on standardized tests, but also in real-life situations.

Pupils who have had the opportunity to practice skills are better able to transfer them to other areas of the curriculum. *Steck-Vaughn Critical Thinking* contains practice pages for every skill presented in the program. Pupils need to know whether or not they are on the right track when they are practicing a new skill. Without feedback, a pupil might continue to practice a skill incorrectly. This program encourages the use of feedback and discussion to help students "think about their thinking."

After pupils begin to consider themselves "thinkers," they will be better able to learn and make use of content area material. Practicing skills such as identifying main ideas, classifying, identifying relationships, thinking about what will happen, and inferring will help students become better readers in the content areas.

Cognitive Skills
The first unit of study is **Knowledge**. This level is considered by many educators to be the first stage in cognitive development. This starting point includes both the acquisition of information and the ability to recall information when needed. The following skills are helpful in developing this stage:
1. Classifying
2. Discriminating Between Real and Make-Believe
3. Discriminating Between Fact and Opinion
4. Discriminating Between Definition and Example
5. Outlining and Summarizing

The second unit of study is **Comprehension**. Comprehension refers to the basic level of understanding and involves the ability to know what is being communicated in order to make use of the information. This includes translating or interpreting a communication or extrapolating information from a communication. The following skills are helpful in developing this stage:
1. Comparing and Contrasting
2. Identifying Structure
3. Identifying Steps in a Process
4. Understanding Pictures
5. Identifying Main Ideas
6. Identifying Relationships

The third unit of study is **Application**. Application is the ability to use a learned skill in a new situation. The following skills are helpful in developing this stage:
1. Ordering Objects
2. Estimating
3. Thinking About What Will Happen
4. Inferring
5. Interpreting Changes in Word Meanings

The fourth unit of study is **Analysis**. Analysis is the ability to break down information into its integral parts and to identify the relationship of each part to the total organization. The following skills are helpful in developing this stage:
1. Judging Completeness
2. Thinking About Facts That Fit
3. Distinguishing Abstract from Concrete
4. Judging Logic of Actions
5. Identifying Parts of a Story
6. Examining Story Logic
7. Recognizing True and False

The fifth unit of study in **Synthesis**. Synthesis is the ability to combine existing elements in order to create something original. The following skills are helpful in developing this stage:
1. Communicating Ideas
2. Planning Projects
3. Building Hypotheses
4. Drawing Conclusions
5. Proposing Alternatives

The sixth unit of study is **Evaluation**. Evaluation involves the ability to make a judgment about the value of something by using a standard. The following skills are helpful in developing this stage:
1. Testing Generalizations
2. Developing Criteria
3. Judging Accuracy
4. Making Decisions
5. Identifying Values
6. Interpreting the Mood of a Story

Features of the Program

Specific skills are listed in the Table of Contents and may be easily found if you need to access a certain skill or area. Each of the 35 skills has been correlated to the content areas of language arts, social studies, science, and math. This chart is on page 4. A letter to parents explaining the goals and benefits of the program is provided on page 5.

The Assessment Test on pages 6-7 may be used to gauge pupils' critical thinking abilities before and after completion of the program. Each unit is also followed by a two-page Assessment Test. The Student Mastery Checklist on page 8 will facilitate your record keeping.

* Bloom, Benjamin. *Taxonomy of Educational Objectives*, Handbook 1: *Cognitive Domain*. New York: David McKay Company, Inc., 1956.

CURRICULUM CORRELATION

Pages	Reading and Language Arts	Social Studies	Science	Math
9-11		✔	✔	
12-13	✔			
14-15	✔			
16-17	✔	✔		
18-19		✔	✔	
22-23	✔		✔	
24-25	✔			
26-27	✔	✔		
28				✔
29-30	✔			
31-32		✔	✔	
33-35	✔	✔		
38-40	✔	✔		✔
41-42				✔
43-44	✔			
45-47	✔			
48-49	✔			
52-53	✔	✔		
54-55		✔		
56	✔			
57-58	✔	✔		
59	✔	✔		
60-61	✔		✔	
62-63	✔			
66-67	✔	✔		
68-69		✔	✔	
70-71	✔			
72-74	✔		✔	✔
75-76	✔	✔		
79-80	✔		✔	
81-82			✔	✔
83-84		✔		
85-87	✔	✔		
88-90	✔	✔	✔	
91-92	✔			

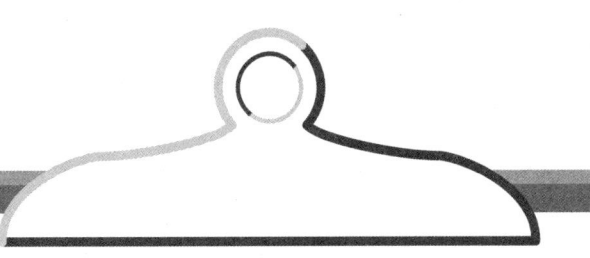

Dear Parent,

Being able to think clearly and to process information in increasingly complex ways is a necessity in the modern world and one of the primary goals of education. This year your child will be using critical thinking exercises to extend his or her ability to read, think, and reason.

The skills we will be practicing are grouped in levels of thinking. These levels are knowledge, comprehension, application, and analysis. The levels are each important. The higher the level of thinking, the more complex the task is. The exercises move from the concrete to the more abstract levels of thinking. We will practice skills such as classifying, identifying main ideas, inferring, and judging completeness.

From time to time, your child may bring home some of these critical thinking practice sheets. To best help your child, please consider the following suggestions:

* Provide a quiet place to work.
* Go over the directions together.
* Show interest in the work.
* Encourage your child to do his or her best.
* Help your child if he or she gets frustrated.
* Check the lesson when it is complete.

Many of these exercises can be easily extended by thinking of similar examples. Your involvement will encourage your child, give you information about how he or she thinks, and provide an opportunity for you to work together. Positive family experiences such as these help promote life-long learning.

Thanks for your help!

Sincerely,

Name _____ Date _____

Assessment Test

This picture was drawn after a marathon race. As you study the picture, imagine that you are the newspaper reporter who will write about the race.

A. Identifying Main Ideas

Write a headline to accompany the picture. Your headline should state the main idea.

_____

B. Comparing and Contrasting

On the lines below, make notes comparing and contrasting the runners shown in the picture.

How the Runners Are Alike	How the Runners Are Different
_____	_____
_____	_____

C. Identifying Relationships

Write a caption to go with the picture. Make up names for the winner and the runners-up. Your caption should show **time relationships** with the words **first**, **next**, and **last**. You might also include a **cause-effect relationship** to explain how the winner won the race.

_____

_____

_____

6   © Steck-Vaughn Company   Critical Thinking 5, SV 6216-4

Name _____ Date _____

Assessment Test (p. 2)

D. Building Hypotheses

The pictures at the bottom of the page show four of the many kinds of animals that migrate.

1. Write a hypothesis telling what may cause some animals to migrate.

   _____
   _____

2. Name some of the sources you would consult to find out whether your hypothesis is correct.

   _____
   _____

E. Planning Projects

Imagine that you have been asked to join an oceanographic expedition to study the migration path of a humpback whale. Describe what specific job you would like to do in this project. Tell about the material and skills you would need.

_____
_____
_____

caribou   **salmon**   **geese**   **whale**

Student Mastery Checklist

Name	Skill # 1	2	3	4	5	6	7	8	9	10	11	12	13	14	15	16	17	18	19	20	21	22	23	24	25	26	27	28	29	30	31	32	33	34	35	Comments

Name _____ Date _____

Unit 1 Knowledge

Classifying

When you classify, you arrange things in groups according to their similarities. Read the following paragraphs and the chart that shows how food is grouped.

What's your favorite food? Is it a plate of spicy spaghetti or a bowl of cool ice cream? Whatever your favorite food, it belongs to one of the food groups in the chart.

Next to each food group is the daily serving size suggested to maintain a healthful diet. You'll notice that food containing fats, oils, and sweets should be eaten sparingly. So do your body a favor—snack on carrots instead of cookies!

Food Group	Servings
A. Bread, Cereal, Rice, and Pasta	6-11
B. Vegetables	3-5
C. Fruits	2-4
D. Milk, Yogurt, and Cheese	2-3
E. Meat, Poultry, Fish, Dry Beans, Eggs, and Nuts	2-3
F. Fats, Oils, and Sweets	Use sparingly.

Source: Food Guide Pyramid, U.S. Department of Agriculture, May 1992.

Classify each food by writing the letter of the food group to which the food belongs.

1. apple _____
2. peanut _____
3. hamburger _____
4. noodles _____
5. cheese _____
6. broccoli _____
7. rice _____
8. butter _____
9. corn flakes _____
10. lettuce _____

If you eat a meal of spaghetti and meatballs with a green salad and a glass of milk, what food groups are included in your meal?

© Steck-Vaughn Company

Critical Thinking 5, SV 6216-4

9

Classifying

Usually, an item can be classified, or categorized, in more than one group. Each person listed below may be categorized as a member of someone's immediate family or as a relative. They also may be categorized as male or female and as members of the same generation or an older generation. Write the name of each person under all the headings of groups to which the person could belong. Some blank lines will not be used. Some answers may be used more than once.

| aunt | cousin | brother | mother | grandmother | uncle |
| stepfather | stepmother | sister | grandfather | father |

Immediate Family

_____   _____
_____   _____
_____   _____

Other Relatives

_____   _____
_____   _____
_____   _____

Male

_____   _____
_____   _____
_____   _____

Female

_____   _____
_____   _____
_____   _____

Same Generation as You

_____   _____
_____   _____
_____   _____
_____   _____

Older Generation than You

_____   _____
_____   _____
_____   _____
_____   _____

Name _____ Date _____

Classifying

Writers often write about kinds, or classes, of things. When you read, you can note how items are classified. Read this article. Then classify each of the instruments mentioned in the article by writing its name under the correct heading below.

Listen to an orchestra, and you'll hear one beautiful, harmonious piece of music. That music is produced by a variety of musical instruments, from big **bass drums** to dainty **piccolos**. **Flutes** sing high melodies, while **tubas** blow low and deep. The delicate **triangle** tinkles, while **cellos** sound mournful. **Violins** produce a wide range of rich sounds.

Although there's a variety of instruments, there are actually only three main kinds of instruments—stringed, wind, and percussion. A stringed instrument produces sound when its strings are plucked or when a bow is moved across them. Just think of the sound you hear when someone strums a **guitar**. A wind instrument is played with the breath. Picture a **trumpet** player blowing into his or her horn. The percussion instruments are played by striking them. Just hear the clang of **cymbals**.

STRINGED	WIND	PERCUSSION
_____	_____	_____
_____	_____	_____
_____	_____	_____
	_____	

To play the piano, you strike the keys. The keys, in turn, strike little hammers that cause strings to vibrate. In which two categories of musical instruments would you classify the piano? Why?

_____

_____

_____

_____

© Steck-Vaughn Company   Critical Thinking 5, SV 6216-4

Name _____ Date _____

Real and Fanciful

Many of the stories you read are **fiction**, or made up by the author. Yet they are usually about people who really could exist and events that really could happen. Some fiction, however, is **fantasy**. It concerns people and events that can only be imagined. Write two different stories—one **realistic** and one fantasy. If only one sentence is given, use it in both stories. For each pair of sentences, use one sentence in each story. Then, on a separate sheet of paper, complete each story with an appropriate ending.

Sentence 1: Daniel sat at the school's new computer and turned it on.

Sentence 2: The computer whirred, buzzed, clicked, and then showed a prompt sign.

Sentence 3: Daniel inserted a disk and hit a few keys.
   or Daniel thought he must be mistaken when he saw the keyboard typing by itself.

Sentence 4: Then Daniel saw this message on the screen: "Wait till you see what I can do!"
   or He had a great idea for a story.

Realistic Story _____

_____

_____

_____

Fantasy _____

_____

_____

_____

Name _____ Date _____

Real and Fanciful

People sometimes exaggerate to express strong feelings. For example, a person who says, "My mouth was on fire when I tasted that food," is reacting strongly to an unpleasant event. A simple statement of fact would be, "The taste of the strong, spicy food caused a burning sensation in my mouth."

Finish each sentence below by underlining the word or words in parentheses that will make the sentence a simple statement of fact.

1. There were (millions of, several, thousands of) mice scurrying around the old house.

2. When the branches of the old tree swayed, they (made a swishing sound, moaned and groaned, scared me to death).

3. The lights over the pond, which were probably caused by (UFO's, prowlers with flashlights, fireflies), gave me an eerie feeling as they twinkled off and on.

4. The winning wrestler won an amazing number of matches during his career. He won (five, 8 million, 105) matches.

5. The room is so cold that the temperature in here must be (zero, cold enough to freeze us to death, near freezing).

6. We saw a waterfall in the river that was (sky high, taller than an ant hill, as high as a redwood tree).

7. The new town hall will be (very beautiful, the finest in the land, the most impressive building in history).

8. The noise from the engine was loud enough to (split our eardrums, drive us crazy, almost deafen us for the moment).

9. My younger brother has grown (very rapidly, like a weed, by leaps and bounds).

© Steck-Vaughn Company   Critical Thinking 5, SV 6216-4

Name _____   Date _____

Fact and Opinion

A **fact** is a statement that you can prove through evidence.

An **opinion** is a statement that represents your belief or judgment, but which you cannot yet prove.

A. Each sentence below contains a fact and an opinion. Put one line under the fact and two lines under the opinion.

1. John bought a new car which he thinks is the best car ever made.

2. Because she felt that she might get a lot of attention, Peg joined the basketball team.

3. Darren and Hank bravely walked into the forest that everyone believed was haunted.

4. "You surely have the most beautiful house in town," Lila said when she came to visit Judy.

5. When the class judged the pictures, most of the students thought Art's drawing was the best.

B. Write **F** before each fact and **O** before each opinion.

_____ 1. Most airplane crashes seem to be the fault of careless traffic controllers.

_____ 2. The process of filling a rubber tire with compressed air was invented in 1888.

_____ 3. Several countries claim ownership of land near the South Pole.

_____ 4. We have the greatest baseball team ever!

_____ 5. I think that plants have emotions and feelings.

Name _____ Date _____

Fact and Opinion

One week last summer, Lisa and Mimi visited their friend Meredith, who lives on a ranch. After the girls returned to their home in the city, they told their parents about the trip. Read the girls' statements below. Write **Fact** before each statement of fact. Write **Opinion** before each opinion.

_____ 1. "The ranch house was red brick with white trim," said Lisa.

_____ 2. "We watched the cowhands brand some calves," Mimi recalled.

_____ 3. "It seems to me that Meredith's family needs more help around the ranch," stated Lisa.

_____ 4. "I think ranch food is much better than the food we eat at home," announced Mimi.

_____ 5. "Meredith's family took us to see a rodeo," said Lisa.

_____ 6. "A rodeo is the most exciting sport in the world to watch!" exclaimed Mimi.

_____ 7. "That was the best vacation I'll ever have for the rest of my life!" announced Lisa.

_____ 8. "I'm definitely going to work on a ranch when I grow up," said Mimi.

_____ 9. "I have a feeling that Meredith's family will invite us back again sometime," said Lisa.

_____ 10. "I've already written and thanked them for showing us such a fine time," said Mimi.

© Steck-Vaughn Company

Critical Thinking 5, SV 6216-4

15

Name _____   Date _____

Definition and Example

A. A **definition** of a word tells the meaning of that word. An **example** gives an illustration of a word. For each word below, choose the best definition and place its letter on the top line. Place the letter of the examples on the bottom line. The first one is done for you.

1. animal   __I__
               __C__

2. country   _____
              _____

3. building   _____
              _____

4. river   _____
              _____

5. spice   _____
              _____

A   pepper, cloves, ginger, nutmeg
B   a structure with four walls, a roof, and a floor
C   cows, sheep, and oxen
D   a large stream of water
E   school, store, home
F   Amazon, Mississippi, Nile
G   Canada, Mexico, Italy, Spain
H   a flavored or scented plant substance
I   any living organism that is not a plant
J   the region of a nation

B. Find the definition of each of these words in a dictionary. Write the definition on the line after **definition**. If the dictionary gives examples, write them on the line after **examples**.

1. **container**   definition: _____
                  examples: _____

2. **fern**   definition: _____
                  examples: _____

3. **cat**   definition: _____
                  examples: _____

© Steck-Vaughn Company   CRITICAL THINKING 5, SV 6216-4

Name _____ Date _____

Definition and Example

A **definition** is the meaning of a word. An **example** is the name of an item that illustrates the word. For each missing word below, a definition and some examples are given. Write **D** before each definition and **E** before each group of examples. Then, unscramble the bold letters to find the word being defined. Write that word on the line at the right. The first one is done for you.

1. __D__ outerwear made of cloth
   __E__ **h**at **co**at gl**o**v**es**   _____clothes_____

2. _____ something to sit on
   _____ chair bench stool   _____

3. _____ vine tree tulip grass
   _____ a living thing that is not an animal   _____

4. _____ something that covers or protects
   _____ **h**ouse tent **s**hed lean-to roof   _____

5. _____ any group of warm-blooded vertebrates with wings
   _____ wren robin starling **d**uck   _____

6. _____ any implement used to do work
   _____ hoe pliers hatchet shovel   _____

7. _____ the condition of the atmosphere
   _____ **w**et **w**indy calm stormy **h**ot breezy   _____

8. _____ nervous joyful **t**ense moody giddy
   _____ a strong feeling   _____

© Steck-Vaughn Company

Critical Thinking 5, SV 6216-4

Name _____ Date _____

Outlining and Summarizing

A **summary** is a statement that briefly gives the main idea of a longer selection.

A. Read the paragraph and the three summaries that follow it. Underline the summary that best explains the main idea of the article. Then explain why you chose that particular summary.

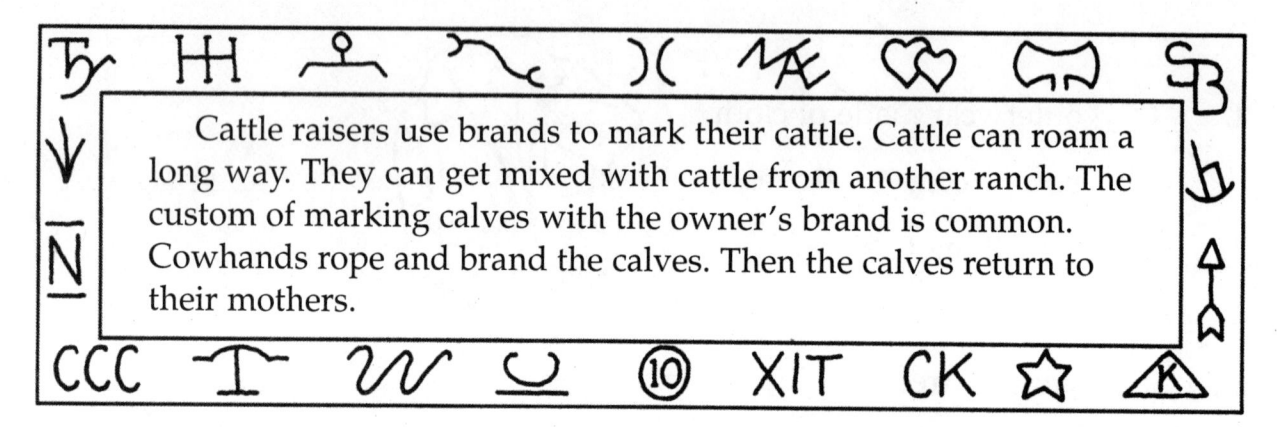

> Cattle raisers use brands to mark their cattle. Cattle can roam a long way. They can get mixed with cattle from another ranch. The custom of marking calves with the owner's brand is common. Cowhands rope and brand the calves. Then the calves return to their mothers.

Summary 1. Branding cattle is not a very kind way to treat animals.
Summary 2. Ranchers brand cattle so that they will not lose the animals.
Summary 3. Many kinds of brands are used by ranchers. These brands help to find lost calves.

_____
_____

B. Read the paragraph below. Then write a summary of it.

Cellulose is the woody part of plants that gives them stiffness. Without cellulose, people would be without thousands of articles they use every day. Cotton fibers, linen cloth, coco matting, and manila rope are largely cellulose. Wood, too, is mostly cellulose, as is the paper that is made from wood. Cellulose is also used in the manufacture of certain plastics.

_____
_____
_____
_____

Name _____ Date _____

Outlining and Summarizing

Read the following article to find out about four kinds of animals. Then fill in the outline, telling what each animal **does** and what it **symbolizes**.

Animals and What They Symbolize

People have always enjoyed comparing animal activity to human behavior. As a result, animals have come to stand for certain things. The bee, for example, works continuously, producing honey and helping flowers grow. People, therefore, feel that the bee stands for hard work.

Spiders suck blood from the insects they trap in their webs. For this reason, spiders have become symbols of misers—people who become wealthy at the expense of others. Another animal, the snail, has come to symbolize laziness, because it moves so slowly.

The butterfly symbolizes the process of life itself. This is because butterflies go through four complete changes in their life cycle—from egg, to caterpillar, to chrysalis, to full-grown butterfly.

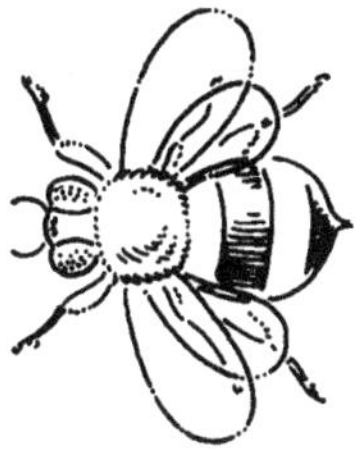

Outline

I. The bee

   A. _____

   B. _____

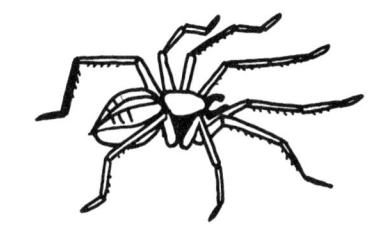

II. The spider

   A. _____

   B. _____

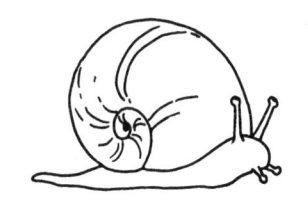

III. The snail

   A. _____

   B. _____

IV. The butterfly

   A. _____

   B. _____

© Steck-Vaughn Company

Critical Thinking 5, SV 6216-4

Name _____ Date _____

Unit 1 Assessment Test

A. Definition and Example

-17- ENVELOPES	-5- HOLIDAY PLACEMATS	-12- CRAYONS	-7- BANNERS	-13- STRING
-4- BALLOONS	-1- PENCILS	-18- FELT-TIP PENS	-10- NOTE PAPER	-19- PADS
-9- GIFT BOXES	-20- LETTER PAPER	-6- WRAPPING PAPER	-2- RIBBON	-14- BALLPOINT PENS
-11- BRUSHES	-3- STREAMERS	-16- CARDS	-15- PAINTS	-8- TAPE

The picture above shows 20 boxes of supplies delivered to a small shop. After each definition below, write the numbers of the boxes that hold examples of the item defined. Some numbers may be placed after more than one definition.

1. **stationery:** material to be written on _____

2. **writing tools:** materials with which marks are made _____

3. **decorations:** materials used as ornaments _____

5. **packaging:** materials used to enclose, wrap, or bundle items _____

B. Outlining

Use your completed activity A above to make an outline of supplies delivered to the store.

_____
_____
_____
_____
_____
_____

Name _____ Date _____

Unit 1 Assessment Test (p. 2)

C. Real and Fanciful

1. In the following paragraph, a writer described **dew**. To help readers picture the dew, the writer used fanciful comparisons. As you read the description, underline the comparisons.

    Little drops of dew sparkle like diamonds as they roll down the power lines like marbles. As the sun rises, the drops blink like traffic lights as they sway on the lines with the early morning breeze.

2. Study the picture of the raging waterfall. Use fanciful comparisons to write a paragraph that describes the waterfall.

   _____
   _____
   _____
   _____
   _____

D. Fact and Opinion

1. Write a sentence that states a fact about the waterfall. _____
   _____
   _____

2. Write a sentence that states your opinion about the waterfall. _____
   _____
   _____

Unit 2 Comprehension
Comparing and Contrasting

To **compare** means to identify **likenesses**. To **contrast** means to identify **differences**.

Blue Jay   Mallard Duck

A. Study the birds shown in the picture.

1. Compare the birds by listing two ways in which they are alike.

   a. _____

   b. _____

2. Contrast the birds by listing two ways in which they are different.

   a. _____

   b. _____

B. Read the following paragraph. Then list two ways in which the hornbill and the mallee fowl are alike and two ways in which they are different.

The African hornbill and the Australian mallee fowl have unusual nest-building habits. The mallee's nest is built of many layers, with each egg resting on a different layer. The hornbill's nest has hardened mud walls. Within these nests, the eggs incubate—the mallee eggs for about seven weeks, and the hornbill eggs for five weeks.

After the two kinds of chicks hatch, both must dig through barriers. The mallee chick must dig through the layers of the nest to the top. The hornbill chick must peck through the hard mud walls to escape.

Likenesses	Differences
1. _____	1. _____
2. _____	2. _____

Name _____   Date _____

Comparing and Contrasting

A. Each sentence group below **compares** two things, or shows how they are alike. On the line after each group, write a sentence which **contrasts** the things, or shows how they are different.

1. A chair and a bed are both furniture. They both have four legs. _____
   _____

2. An auditorium is designed for recreation, as is a gymnasium. Both are large and hold many people. _____
   _____

3. Pins and needles are both used for sewing. They are small, sharp objects meant to hold material together. _____
   _____

4. Diamonds and iron are both hard. Both must be brought out from mines.
   _____

B. For each pair of items below, write a sentence to tell how the items are alike.

1. A tractor and a pair of roller skates _____
   _____

2. A tree and an umbrella _____
   _____

3. A diary and a telephone _____
   _____

4. A guitar and a bird _____
   _____

© Steck-Vaughn Company

Critical Thinking 5, SV 6216-4

23

Identifying Structure

A **cinquain** is a special kind of five-line poem. A cinquain may follow either of the forms, or structures, described on this page.

A. Study the cinquain at the bottom of the page. Decide which structure it follows. Then copy the cinquain on the five lines next to the structure.

B. On the remaining five lines, write your cinquain, following the cinquain structure next to it.

Structure I

Line 1: one noun stating the subject _____

Line 2: two adjectives describing the noun _____

Line 3: three action verbs _____

Line 4: four words showing feeling about the subject _____

Line 5: another word for the word in Line 1 _____

Structure II

Line 1: two syllables naming the subject _____

Line 2: four syllables describing the subject _____

Line 3: six syllables showing action _____

Line 4: eight syllables showing feeling about the subject _____

Line 5: two syllables that stand for the word or words in Line 1 _____

```
My hat
Fuzzy, warm, soft
Protects, covers, cuddles
Makes a whirl of color on snow
Ski cap
```

Name _____ Date _____

Identifying Structure

Letters make up the structure of a written word. In the word games below, you will play with the structure of words to form other words. In both games, you will be forming **synonyms**, or words that have almost the same meaning.

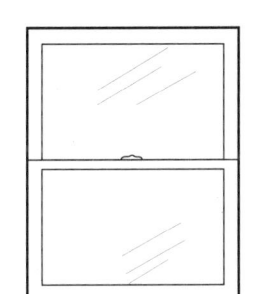

A. In each word pair below, take a letter from the top word and place it in the bottom word to make a pair of synonyms. Keep the letters of the bottom word in the same order. The first pair has been done for you.

1. leash __lash__   3. boast _____   5. turns _____
   bat   __beat__   hip   _____   pin   _____

2. stalk _____   4. furry _____   6. quiet _____
   peak _____   age   _____   lave _____

B. Change the order of the letters in both words of each pair below to form pairs of synonyms. The first pair has been done for you.

1. cork __rock__   4. heat _____   8. peels _____
   notes __stone__   tested _____   pan   _____

2. strut _____   5. paws _____   9. fare _____
   lyre _____   tread _____   dared _____

3. stop _____   6. carve _____   10. least _____
   saint _____   reside _____   orb   _____

                          7. leap _____
                             grin _____

© Steck-Vaughn Company   Critical Thinking 5, SV 6216-4

Name _____ Date _____

Steps in a Process

A. The pictures below make a cartoon. They are similar to a filmstrip. On the lines below the pictures, write what you think is happening in each picture.

1.
2.
3.
4.
5.
6.

1. _____
2. _____
3. _____
4. _____
5. _____
6. _____

B. In which picture is humor first introduced? _____ Why is it humorous? _____
_____

C. Is this a real or fanciful situation? _____

Why? _____

26 © Steck-Vaughn Company   Critical Thinking 5, SV 6216-4

Name _____   Date _____

Steps in a Process

Read the paragraphs below to learn the steps used to make maple syrup. On the lines below the paragraphs, use your own words to tell the steps in order. There are six steps. The first one is given to help you get started.

Maple syrup is made from the sap of sugar maple trees. These trees are found in the northeastern United States and in Canada. To collect the sap, farmers bore holes into the tree trunks about four feet from the ground. Small metal or plastic spouts are forced into the holes. Buckets are hung from the spouts to collect sap as it flows from the holes.

The sap is poured into large tanks and is moved by sleds to a sap house. There, a machine called an evaporator boils the sap until some of the water is evaporated. The remaining liquid is maple syrup.

1. Bore holes into tree trunks. _____

2. _____

3. _____

4. _____

5. _____

6. _____

© Steck-Vaughn Company

Critical Thinking 5, SV 6216-4

Name _____   Date _____

Figural Relationships

Figure and **figural** are words that refer to such things as charts, diagrams, and symbols. Such figures can help you see and understand quickly how facts are related.

A. Study the **bar graph** below. Then complete the sentences that follow it.

POINTS MADE IN A GAME

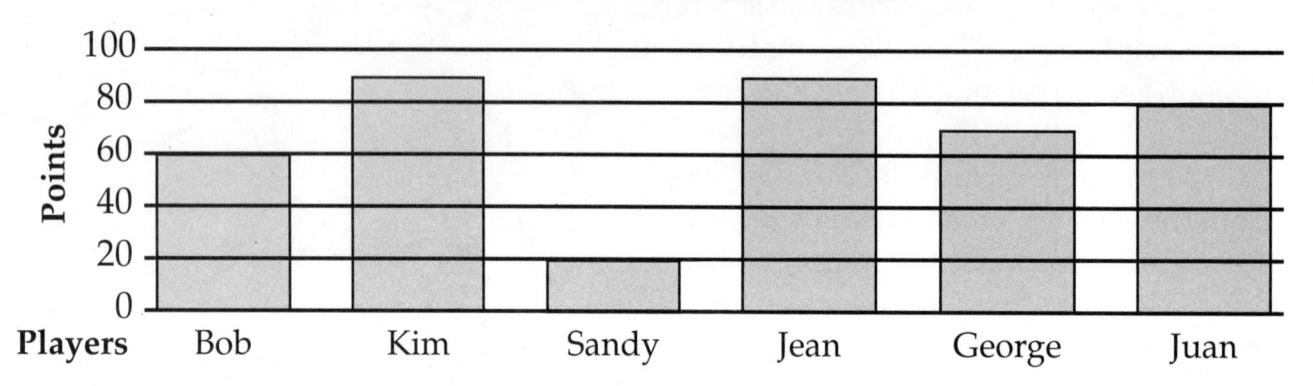

Player	Points
Bob	60
Kim	90
Sandy	20
Jean	90
George	70
Juan	80

1. _____ and _____ tied for first place.

2. _____ came in second, with a score of _____.

3. _____ got 40 fewer points than _____ did.

B. The line graph below shows George's scores for six different games. Study the graph. Then complete the sentences and answer the question that follows.

POINTS SCORED BY GEORGE

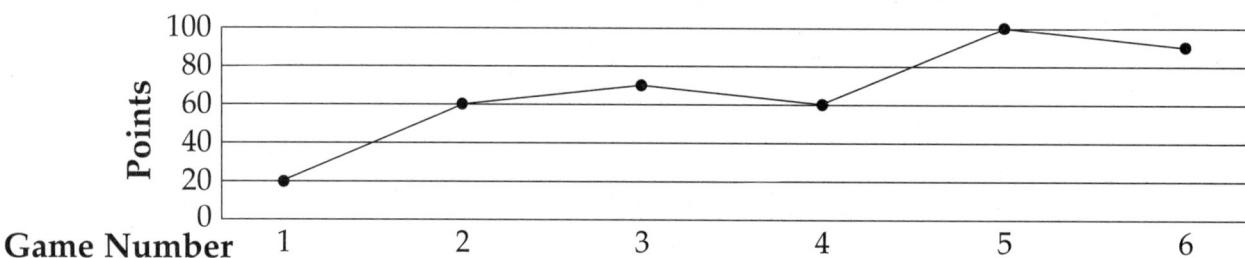

Game Number	Points
1	20
2	60
3	70
4	60
5	100
6	90

1. George got his highest score in _____.

2. The first time he played, George's score was _____.

3. George's scores were the same in games _____ and _____.

4. In general, did George improve, get worse, or stay about the same as he played the game? _____

© Steck-Vaughn Company   Critical Thinking 5, SV 6216-4

Name _____ Date _____

Comparing Word Meanings

Read the words in each group below. Then find the word in the **Word List** that is related to each word in the group and write it on the line. The first one is done for you.

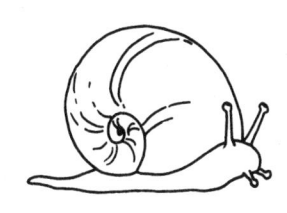

Word List

wheel
story
key
shell
pen
ring
teeth
light
pin
plate
nail
glass
bed
star
table

____pin____ 1. straight, safety, bowling, clothes, rolling

_____ 2. pig, ball-point, bull, play

_____ 3. wagon, steering, potter's, ship's, spinning

_____ 4. circus, boxing, tree, bathtub, telephone

_____ 5. sea, egg, pie, snail

_____ 6. movie, general's, shooting, lucky

_____ 7. false, gear, saw, rake, comb

_____ 8. mystery, picture, short, news

_____ 9. home, dinner, paper, license

_____ 10. hospital, flower, water, rock

_____ 11. spy, eye, field, drinking, window

_____ 12. piano, musical, lock, answer, code

_____ 13. multiplication, dining, time

_____ 14. night, flash, sun, sky

_____ 15. finger, toe, roofing, finishing, six-penny

© Steck-Vaughn Company

Critical Thinking 5, SV 6216-4

29

Comparing Word Meanings

Below are two games of Word Tic-Tac-Toe. In each bracket, a word is printed above the line: | huge . Pick a synonym for the word from the list below. Write the synonym below the word: | huge . The first player | large to complete a row of brackets across, up and down, or diagonally is the winner. Not all of the words will be used.

Synonym Search Box

- hug
- qualified
- elect
- mislay
- tumult
- miniature
- radiant
- rapid
- reaction
- ready
- genuine
- violin
- reap
- revolt
- restore
- remember
- still
- sensation
- foolish
- show
- tremble
- vanish
- surprise
- vague
- accentuate
- expire
- ragged

GAME I

emphasize	embrace	eligible
elapse	misplace	shining
choose	uproar	tattered

GAME II

swift	real	rebuild
response	harvest	recall
prepared	rebellion	thrilling

Name _____ Date _____

Identifying Main Ideas

A good paragraph is built around a **main idea**. Often, this main idea is stated in a **topic sentence**. At other times, there is no topic sentence, though the facts in the paragraph are still clustered around a main idea.

A. Read each paragraph below. If the paragraph has a topic sentence, underline that sentence.

1. One hero of the First World War was a pigeon that carried an important message through artillery fire. During the Second World War, the British dropped boxes of homing pigeons behind enemy lines. Pigeons were also used to carry messages during the Korean War.

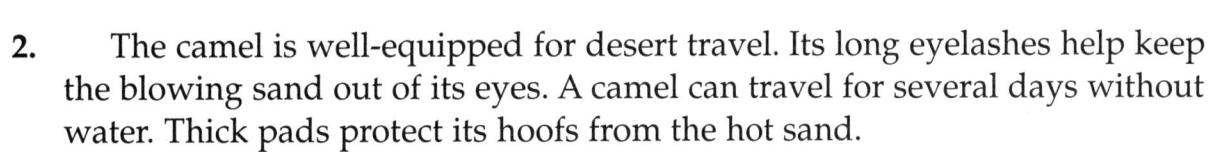

2. The camel is well-equipped for desert travel. Its long eyelashes help keep the blowing sand out of its eyes. A camel can travel for several days without water. Thick pads protect its hoofs from the hot sand.

3. A hippopotamus can run on the bottom of a lake or river at eight miles an hour. On land, it can run as fast as a human. This large animal is a fast swimmer and can dive, sink like a rock, or float like a log.

4. Though insects are small, many of them can cause great damage. Some insects can destroy crops. Others can cause various illnesses in people and in other animals.

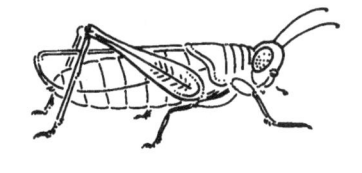

B. A good title states the main idea briefly and in an interesting way. On the following lines, write a title for each paragraph above.

1. _____
2. _____
3. _____
4. _____

© Steck-Vaughn Company

Critical Thinking 5, SV 6216-4

Name _____ Date _____

Identifying Main Ideas

Read each group of sentences below. Decide which sentence seems unrelated to the others, and draw a line through it. Then think of a **main idea**, or **topic sentence**, that could be used to introduce the remaining three sentences. Write a paragraph using your topic sentence and following it with the three related sentences.

A. 1. Native Americans could tell direction in the forest by examining where moss grew.

2. Broken branches and twigs were clues to the paths taken by forest animals.

3. Native Americans told a variety of myths and legends.

4. Keen ears could pick up the special sounds made by different birds and mammals.

_____
_____
_____
_____

B. 1. The investigations of scientists have led to the cures for many diseases.

2. Scientists hold conventions frequently.

3. A scientist's patient investigations can also unfold important facts about the earth and about the universe.

4. The results of any investigation lead to new and fascinating questions which may be answered by further study.

_____
_____
_____
_____

Name _____   Date _____

Identifying Relationships

Events are often related in **time**. Often, words such as **then**, **next**, or **as** are clues that let you know the time order that relates the events.

Read the sentences below and follow these three steps.

A. Circle the clue word or phrase that shows the time relationship between the events.

B. If one event happened before the other, underline the part of the sentence that tells what happened first.

C. If both events happened at the same time, put a check on the line before the sentence.

_____ 1. When Jim drove the car into the driveway, he noticed that the garage door was open.

_____ 2. He carefully eased out from under the wheel, after parking the car.

_____ 3. Before he even opened the door to the house, Jim could tell that something strange was going on.

_____ 4. As Jim entered the kitchen, he heard odd noises coming from the living room.

_____ 5. He was not frightened until the noises got louder.

_____ 6. He hesitated, and then walked bravely through the kitchen to the hall.

_____ 7. Outside the living room, Jim's heart pounded while the strange noises continued.

_____ 8. After deciding to look now or never, Jim yanked the door open.

_____ 9. When he looked around, Jim was surprised to see only his father with some friends.

_____ 10. Looking puzzled, Jim stepped into the room and then smiled with relief.

_____ 11. At the same moment, Jim's father turned on some new electronic drum machines.

_____ 12. After Jim's excitement was over, his father showed him how to use the drum machines.

© Steck-Vaughn Company   Critical Thinking 5, SV 6216-4

Name _____ Date _____

Identifying Relationships

Events are often related because one event causes the other to happen. This is called a **cause-effect** relationship. Clue words such as **because**, **since**, and **as a result** often signal a cause-effect relationship.

A. Read the following paragraphs. In each blank, write a clue word or phrase which points out the cause-effect relationship between the events.

1. Before the invention of the steam engine, ships used the power of the wind to move across the seas. It took from three to four weeks to sail from America to Europe. _____ the winds generally blew from west to east, it took longer to go from Europe to America.

2. During the last century, pioneers began to have a difficult time finding vast stretches of land in the East. _____, they started to travel westward across the country in covered wagons.

3. Seashell collecting was once a popular hobby. _____ many varieties of seashells have now become rare, ecologists are discouraging people from continuing this hobby.

B. Complete each sentence to make it show a cause-effect relationship.

1. The team won the tournament because _____
   _____.

2. Our field trip was a success because _____
   _____.

3. Since it is beginning to snow, our trip to the mountains _____
   _____.

4. New speed-limit laws were passed, and, as a result, _____
   _____.

34 © Steck-Vaughn Company   Critical Thinking 5, SV 6216-4

Identifying Relationships

The first two sentences in each group below tell about events that at first do not seem to be related to one another. The third sentence, however, tells about an event that was caused by the first two. On the lines below each sentence group, explain the cause-effect relationship.

1. Mrs. Brown bought a toy in New York. Six-year-old Vivian lived in London. Vivian played with her new toy.

2. Mountains near the town of Troy received heavy rainfall. In the valley some miles away was a small stream. Rather suddenly the small stream flooded.

3. Mr. and Mrs. Roberts were robbed one dark night. Jane Roberts was away at college, studying accounting. Jane began to look for a job.

4. The price of gasoline rose a great deal. Yuji works in a city several miles from his home. Yuji now rides to work with three other people.

5. Several stores suddenly closed. The power company moved to another town. The school enrollment dropped.

Name _____ Date _____

Unit 2 Assessment Test

This picture was done after a marathon race. As you study the picture, imagine that you are the newspaper reporter who will write about the race.

A. Identifying Main Ideas

Write a headline to accompany the picture. Your headline should state the main idea.

_____

B. Comparing and Contrasting

On the lines below, make notes comparing and contrasting the runners shown in the picture.

How the Runners Are Alike	How the Runners Are Different
_____	_____
_____	_____

C. Identifying Relationships

Write a caption to go with the picture. Make up names for the winner and the runners-up. Your caption should show **time relationships** with the words **first**, **next**, and **last**. You might also include a **cause-effect relationship** to explain how the winner won the race.

_____
_____
_____
_____

36   © Steck-Vaughn Company   Critical Thinking 5, SV 6216-4

Name _____ Date _____

Unit 2 Assessment Test (p. 2)

Refer to the figure as you complete the following activities.

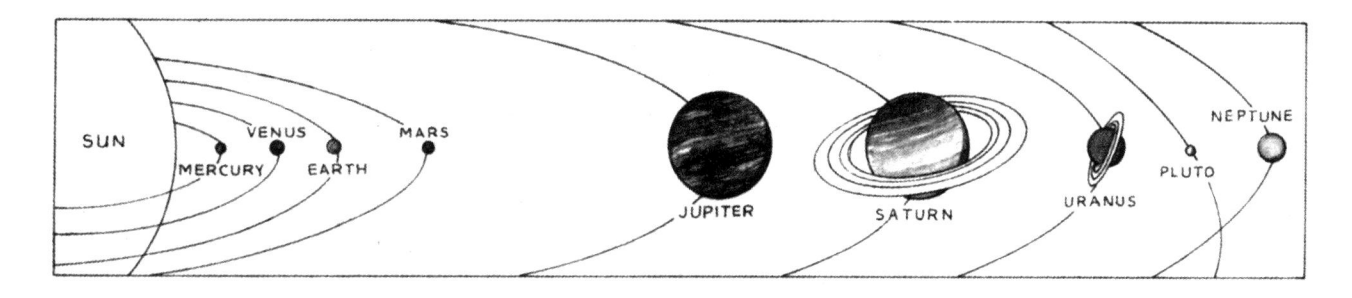

D. Figural Relationships

Which main heavenly bodies make up the solar system? Which body lies at the center of the solar system? How do the other bodies move around it?

_____

_____

_____

E. Comparing and Contrasting

How does the size of the planets farther from the sun compare with the size of the planets closer to it? _____

_____

F. Identifying Relationships

What position from the sun is Earth? Does Earth lie between Venus and the sun, or does Venus lie between Earth and the sun? Does Pluto ever lie between Neptune and the sun?

_____

_____

© Steck-Vaughn Company   Critical Thinking 5, SV 6216-4   **37**

Name _____ Date _____

Unit 3
Ordering Objects

Objects can be put in different **orders**, according to the standard you are using. In the activities below, you will use two different standards for ordering objects.

A. Number the words in each column from **1** to **6** according to the number of syllables each word contains.

1	2	3
_____ information	_____ restriction	_____ cottonwood
_____ outward	_____ electronically	_____ automatically
_____ source	_____ ocean	_____ cough
_____ mathematically	_____ invisibly	_____ fiddle
_____ photograph	_____ fair	_____ grammatical
_____ organization	_____ superintendent	_____ metropolitan

B. Arrange the figures below in order according to the size of the shaded parts. Write **1** on the line below the figure with the smallest shaded part and continue numbering until the largest part is numbered **8**.

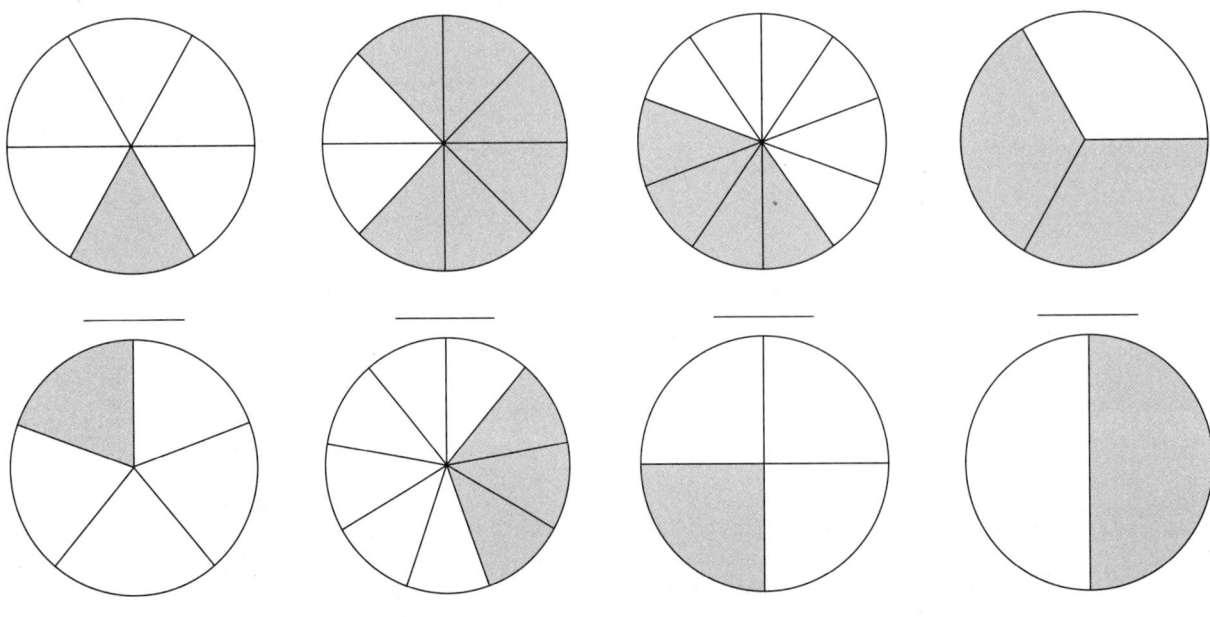

Name _____ Date _____

Ordering Objects

A. Number each column of objects from the thinnest to the thickest. Write **1** before the thinnest. Continue until the thickest is labeled **3**. The first column is done for you.

1	2	3
__2__ pamphlet	_____ rope	_____ branch
__3__ book	_____ string	_____ trunk
__1__ paper	_____ thread	_____ twig

B. In the groups below, order the objects according to weight. Use **1** for the lightest, **3** for the heaviest, and **2** for the object that is in between.

_____ dog	_____ quart	_____ ton
_____ mouse	_____ pint	_____ gram
_____ elephant	_____ gallon	_____ kilogram

C. Think of two different standards you could use to order the objects at the bottom of the page. Then write the different standards on the column-heading lines and list the objects.

Standard 1: _____   Standard 2: _____

_____   _____

_____   _____

_____   _____

_____   _____

Name _____   Date _____

Ordering Objects

A. List the products below according to their importance to human life, their cost, and their durability (how long they last).

| television | bread | car | bed | house | piano | light bulb |

1 Most important first	2 Most expensive first	3 Longest lasting first

B. List some animals that are useful to humans and explain the uses. When your list is complete, number from the most useful animal to the least.

Animal	Uses

Name _____ Date _____

Estimating

An **estimate** is a rough judgment about how long or large something is or about how long it will take to accomplish a task. While an estimate is not exact, it is somewhat more reliable than a **guess**. That is because an estimate is based on some kind of standard, such as a picture, a scale, a key, or our own experience.

Study the map of the United States and the key. Then on the chart below the map, write your estimates of the distance between the various cities shown on the map. An estimate of the distance between Miami and Seattle has already been given to help you get started.

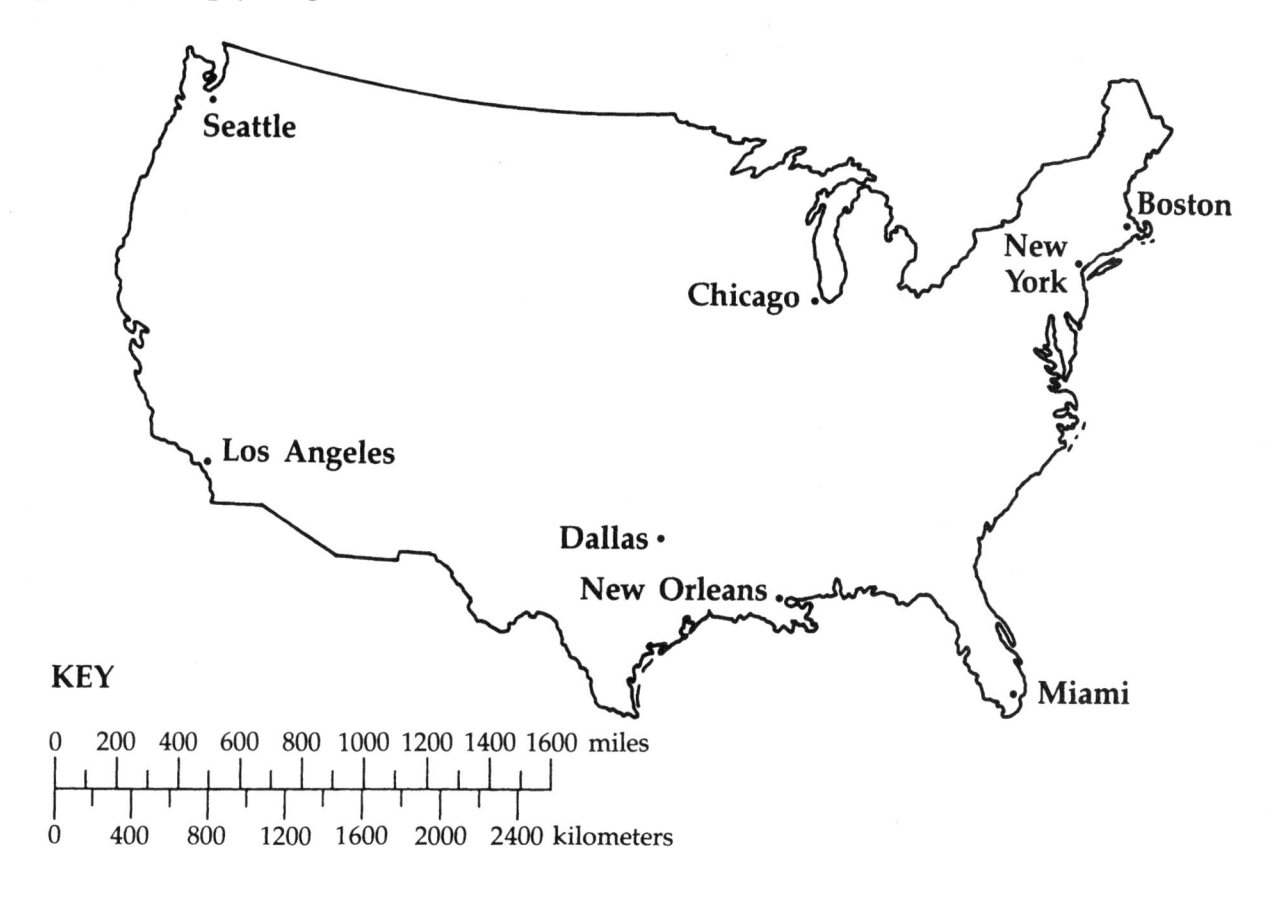

KEY

0   200   400   600   800   1000   1200   1400   1600 miles

0   400   800   1200   1600   2000   2400 kilometers

	Boston	New Orleans	Chicago	Seattle
New York				
Miami				3200 mi (5100 km)
Los Angeles				
Dallas				

© Steck-Vaughn Company

Critical Thinking 5, SV 6216-4

Name _____   Date _____

Estimating

A. Estimate the amount of time it would take **you**—working at the top of your form—to do each of the following chores:

1. paint a gate for your fence _____

2. wash breakfast dishes for a family of four _____

3. buy a three-day supply of groceries _____

4. read 20 pages in a history book _____

5. clean out a small aquarium _____

6. write a composition about autumn _____

B. Now imagine that you have been asked to do all the tasks listed above in a single day. On the chart below, make a schedule. In the right-hand column, list the chores in the order in which you would prefer to do them. In the column at the left, show as closely as possible—in hours and minutes—when you would begin the task and when you would probably finish it. For example, you might write 8 A.M. — 8:30 A.M. to show the time span for doing a chore.

Time	Chore

© Steck-Vaughn Company

Critical Thinking 5, SV 6216-4

Name _____   Date _____

Anticipating Probabilities

A **probability** is something that is very likely to happen. For example, if you do not water a plant for a long time, it is **probable** that the plant will die.

A. Complete each sentence below by telling what the **probable** outcome will be.

1. If it does not rain for some time, it is probable that _____ _____.

2. If the school band practices hard every day, it is probable that the band concert _____ _____.

3. If a player throws a ball at the basketball hoop 100 times, it is probable that _____ _____.

4. If you forget to bring your lunch to school, it is probable that _____ _____.

B. A situation may have more than one probable outcome. Read about the situations below. Then list two probable outcomes for each situation.

1. Mary and Ian are scheduled to play a piano duet on Friday. They are both excellent players, but they have practiced very little together. Mary and Ian will probably

   a. _____.
   b. _____.

2. Leon is very shy. He has worked very hard to learn Spanish. As a result, he has been offered a chance to live with a family in Latin America this summer, along with students from other schools who have done well in Spanish. Leon will probably

   a. _____.
   b. _____.

© Steck-Vaughn Company   Critical Thinking 5, SV 6216-4   **43**

Name _____ Date _____

Anticipating Probabilities

You know that a **probability** is something that is very likely to happen. A **possibility**, on the other hand, is something that **might** or **could** happen if certain other conditions happen, too.

A. Read each sentence below. Then write **probability** or **possibility** on the line before the sentence.

1. _____ This week, someone in your class will get a score of 90 or above on a paper or test.

2. _____ This winter, areas of the Northeast will get heavy snowfalls and high winds.

3. _____ This year, a severe earthquake will hit the area in which you live.

4. _____ Within the next ten years, intelligent beings from another galaxy will visit Earth.

5. _____ Within the next ten years, all the nations of the Western Hemisphere will unite to form one nation.

B. Select two of the sentences in part A which you have labeled **possibility**. On the lines below, tell what you would **probably** do or how your life would **probably** change if such an event actually happened.

1. _____
_____
_____
_____

2. _____
_____
_____
_____

© Steck-Vaughn Company

Critical Thinking 5, SV 6216-4

Name _____ Date _____

Inferring

To **infer** means to reach a conclusion based on what you observe or the facts you have at hand.

Study the picture of the house. Examine the details carefully. Then write a paragraph to tell what you **infer** about the house. For example, do you infer that the house is empty or occupied? Do you infer that people in the neighborhood like or dislike this particular house? For each inference that you make, give at least one picture detail that has led you to that inference. *(detail from the picture)*

_____
_____
_____
_____
_____
_____
_____

© Steck-Vaughn Company   Critical Thinking 5, SV 6216-4   **45**

Name _____   Date _____

Inferring

Many times, an inference is correct. You have enough facts at hand to lead you logically to the correct conclusion. At other times, however, an inference may **not** be correct. As you gather additional information, your inference may change. You may come to a different conclusion.

Here are some facts that may lead you to change your inference about the house you studied on page 45:

- The owner, Mr. M., is old and ill.
- Mr. M.'s wife and other close relatives died sometime ago.
- Mr. M. is extremely shy.
- Mr. M. has very little money.

1. On the basis of the facts above, write a few sentences that explain the condition of the house shown in the picture on page 45.

   _____
   _____
   _____

2. On the basis of the facts above, what would you infer about the kinds of things that Mr. M. needs most?

   _____
   _____
   _____

3. In many cases, it is important to check further to make sure an inference is correct. How would you check to see whether the inference you made in number 2 is correct?

   _____
   _____
   _____
   _____

Name _____ Date _____

Inferring

Read the following paragraphs from a story. Try to fill in information that you are not directly told about the characters in the story. Then complete the exercise that follows.

Jana pushed hard with all her might. Tony could do nothing to help her but give words of encouragement. "One more push, and I think the wheel will come free. Just one more." Finally, one more hard push did it. The right wheel lifted out of the rut between the sidewalk and lawn with a jerk. Tony lurched forward, almost falling out.

"Phew! Sorry about that!" Jana panted.

"That's all right," Tony replied.

"We'll have to tell Dad about that sidewalk so he can fix it," Jana said.

The two proceeded up the walk. Thank goodness for the ramp that led past the front steps to the door of the house. Jana noticed the curtains were drawn. She wondered why, on such a nice, sunny day. After all, her father loved nice, sunshiny days.

Jana opened the front door, then got behind Tony to push him into the house. The darkness inside startled her. It took a few moments for her eyes to adjust. Then she thought she saw shapes rising up and moving toward her—human shapes. Suddenly she heard a huge shout: "Surprise!"

Now put an **X** before each detail you could probably infer is true from reading the story. (3)

_____ 1. Tony is in a wheelchair.

_____ 2. Tony was in a car accident.

_____ 3. Jana and Tony are brother and sister.

_____ 4. Jana is older than Tony.

_____ 5. Jana and Tony live on a farm.

_____ 6. It is summer.

_____ 7. People are throwing a surprise party.

_____ 8. The curtains were drawn so that Jana could not see inside.

_____ 9. Tony knew about the party.

_____ 10. Tony and Jana do not live with their mother.

Name _____ Date _____

Changes in Word Meanings

We often understand the meaning of a word only when we hear or read it in **context**—that is, in connection with other words. This is true of even simple words, such as **trunk**. **Trunk** can mean (1) part of a tree, (2) part of an elephant, or (3) a large container in which to pack clothes or other belongings.

A. Above the word **trunk** in the sentence below, write the number of the meaning that applies to it.

The elephant picked up the trunk with his trunk and set it next to the trunk of the banyan tree.

B. Study each sentence and the underlined words in it. Then rewrite the sentence, replacing one of the underlined words with a word or phrase that has a similar meaning. You may use a dictionary.

1. He had the ill <u>fortune</u> of losing his <u>fortune</u> in the stock market.

   _____
   _____

2. She was not the <u>type</u> to <u>type</u> for long hours at a time.

   _____
   _____

3. At the <u>peak</u> of his career, the explorer went to the <u>peak</u> of Mt. Everest.

   _____
   _____

4. She will <u>study</u> this at home in her <u>study</u>.

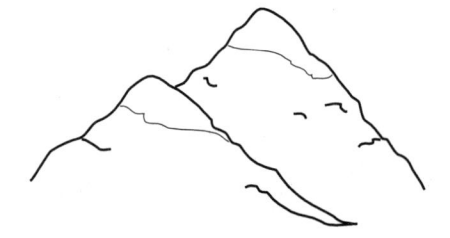

   _____
   _____

48 © Steck-Vaughn Company   Critical Thinking 5, SV 6216-4

Name _____ Date _____

Changes in Word Meanings

A. A simple word—such as *run*—often can be combined with other words to form a phrase that has a special meaning. Read each sentence below and the expressions that follow it. Then, in the blank, write the expression that most sensibly fits the context of the sentence.

1. It is always pleasant to _____ a friend.

   a. run over   **b.** run out of   **c.** run into

2. The detective _____ the man's alibi.

   a. saw through   **b.** saw off   **c.** saw out

3. Midway through the race, Leonard _____.

   a. fell under   **b.** fell behind   **c.** fell off

4. The crowd _____ in amazement as the magician performed.

   a. looked out   **b.** looked on   **c.** looked over

5. In her appearance, Susan _____ her mother.

   a. takes after   **b.** takes over   **c.** takes to

B. In the first column below, copy the expressions you used in the sentences in part A. In the second column, write the meaning of that expression. You may use a dictionary.

Expression	Meaning
1. _____	_____
2. _____	_____
3. _____	_____
4. _____	_____
5. _____	_____

© Steck-Vaughn Company   Critical Thinking 5, SV 6216-4

Name _____ Date _____

Unit 3 Assessment Test

A. Ordering Objects
   Estimating

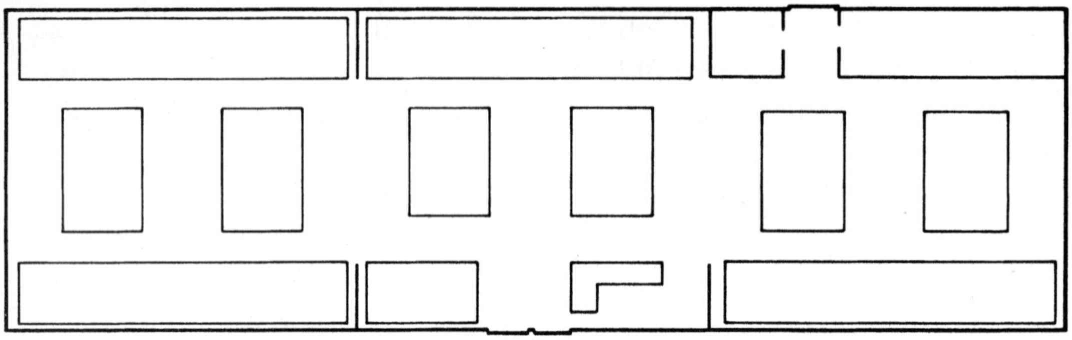

[floor plan diagram with BACKDOOR at top right and ENTRANCE at bottom center]

Mr. and Mrs. White have just bought a row of three stores. One is a stationery shop, one is a gift shop, and one is a hardware store. The Whites have combined the shops to make one large store which sells stationery, gifts, and hardware.

On the floor plan above, write labels to show how you would arrange and order the various items. Keep in mind that customers need to find the things they want easily and that the store must also look attractive and appealing.

Suppose that it is now October 1. The Whites have announced that the new store will open on October 12. On the lines list the tasks that must be carried out before the store can open.

_____
_____
_____
_____
_____

B. Inferring

To buy and combine three stores is a big project. What inference can you make about the Whites and the town they live in?

_____
_____
_____
_____

Name _____ Date _____

Unit 3 Assessment Test (p. 2)

C. Anticipating Probabilities

On opening day, Mr. White gave copies of the following memo to all the employees. Read the memo. Then, on the lines below it, tell two **probable** feelings or reactions the employees would have.

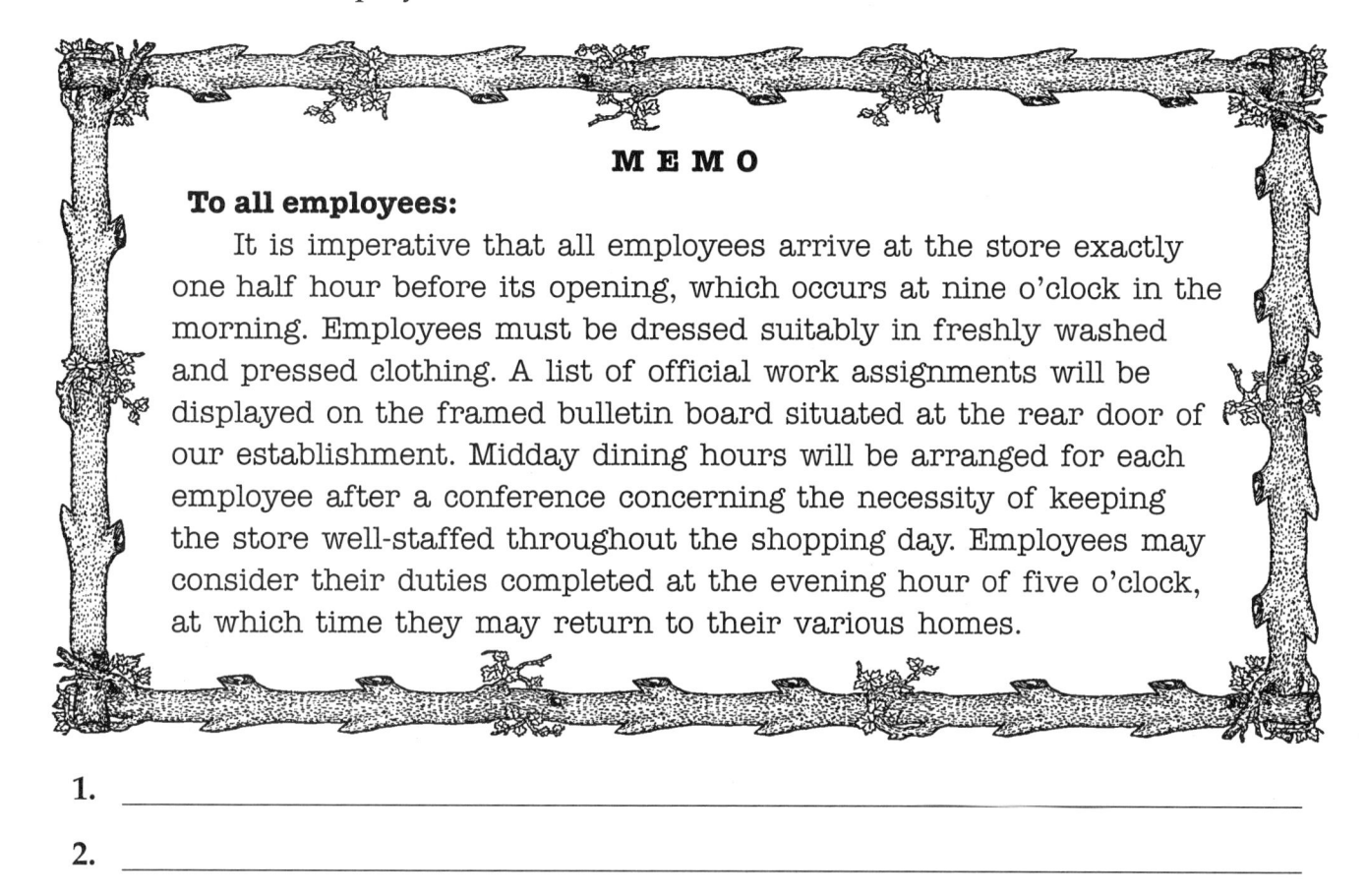

MEMO

To all employees:

It is imperative that all employees arrive at the store exactly one half hour before its opening, which occurs at nine o'clock in the morning. Employees must be dressed suitably in freshly washed and pressed clothing. A list of official work assignments will be displayed on the framed bulletin board situated at the rear door of our establishment. Midday dining hours will be arranged for each employee after a conference concerning the necessity of keeping the store well-staffed throughout the shopping day. Employees may consider their duties completed at the evening hour of five o'clock, at which time they may return to their various homes.

---

1. _____
2. _____

D. Changes in Word Meanings

Mrs. White agreed with the rules in Mr. White's memo, but she felt that the memo was too wordy. She wants the memo rewritten so it is brief and clear. On the lines below, rewrite the memo in a way that would please Mrs. White.

_____

_____

_____

_____

Name _____ Date _____

Unit 4 Analysis
Judging Completeness

When you are asked to perform a task, you need certain details in order to do the task correctly and efficiently. Imagine that you are in the following situations. Tell what you need to know before you can complete each task well.

1. You work in a department store. A customer asks for a bicycle wheel. You need to know _____

_____

_____

2. You work in a hardware store. A customer wants a new lawn mower and would like to have it delivered. You need to know _____

_____

_____

3. Your school principal has asked your class to organize a school art show. Your class needs to know _____

_____

_____

4. Your teacher has asked you to write a composition. You need to know

_____

_____

_____

5. Your parents have asked you to help organize a birthday party for a younger child. You need to know _____

_____

_____

Name _____ Date _____

Judging Completeness

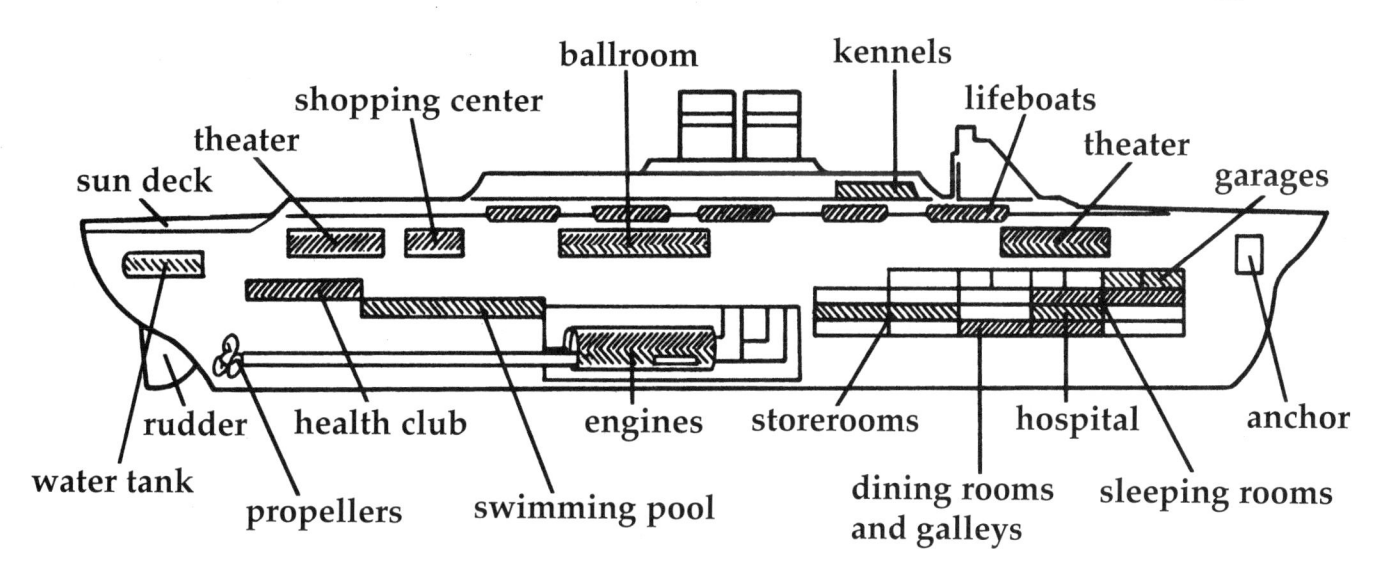

[Diagram of ocean liner cross-section with labels: sun deck, theater, shopping center, ballroom, kennels, lifeboats, theater, garages, water tank, rudder, health club, propellers, engines, swimming pool, storerooms, dining rooms and galleys, hospital, sleeping rooms, anchor]

Cruise ships, or ocean liners, are huge seagoing hotels. There are often as many as a thousand workers, or crew, aboard to provide for the comfort, safety, and health of the passengers. Ocean liners can travel across the Atlantic over eight times before stopping for fuel, water, or supplies. Their galleys, or kitchens, can prepare meals which serve 9,000 daily.

Study the drawing of the ocean liner and read the paragraph. The sentences below refer the drawing. Put a **T** before each sentence which is true according to the drawing. Put **F** before each sentence which is not true according to the drawing.

_____ 1. There is a place to get a haircut on the ship.

_____ 2. The drawing shows where the fuel is stored.

_____ 3. Two people could attend different movies at the same time.

_____ 4. Passengers may transport their cars across the ocean on this ship.

_____ 5. There are escape boats for the passengers in case of emergency.

_____ 6. The swimming pool is on the sun deck.

_____ 7. There is a special place for people who become ill.

_____ 8. Passengers may bring their dogs on this voyage.

_____ 9. There is a flight deck where planes can land on the ship.

© Steck-Vaughn Company   Critical Thinking 5, SV 6216-4   **53**

Relevance of Information

When information is **relevant**, it is important to the subject you are studying. **Relevant** information is to the point.

For each activity below, underline the **two** information sources that would provide you with the most relevant information.

1. You want to find a recipe for upside-down cake.
   recipe book   cookbook   magazine   newspaper

2. You want to know how to bandage a deep cut.
   magazine   science book   health book   first-aid book

3. You would like to learn how to grow zinnias.
   gardening book   book on shrubs   book on soil   instructions on a package of zinnia seeds

4. You need to know the names of the planets in our solar system.
   health book   astronomy book   astrology book   science book

5. You want to know how to spell and pronounce the word *pecuniary*.
   atlas   spelling book   dictionary   newspaper

6. You would like to become informed about different careers.
   social studies book   individual books describing careers   newspaper articles   counseling books

7. You need to improve your handwriting.
   chart on cursive letters   spelling book   English book   handwriting book

8. You are interested in the duties of nurses.
   hospital manual   health book   book about careers   book of medical diseases

9. You are interested in the most recent scientific discoveries.
   science book   newspaper   encyclopedia   recent science magazines

Name _____ Date _____

Relevance of Information

Suppose that you are to write a report about life in the Amazon region of South America. From the 12 sentences below, choose the ten that you think are most relevant to the subject. Then organize the ten sentences into a paragraph, rewording where necessary.

1. Malaria is more common in tropical areas than in other places.
2. Mosquito netting is necessary equipment in this region.
3. Due to flooding and poor soil, the region does not have good farmland.
4. Large parts of the Amazon rain forest are disappearing.
5. The sun can cause serious sunburn even on a cloudy day.
6. Tropical rainfall is heavy and frequent.
7. Tropical rivers contain anacondas, alligators, and piranha.
8. The climate of equatorial regions is hot and humid all year.
9. Salt tablets may help to maintain body fluids in hot climates.
10. Boiling is one way to purify water for drinking.
11. A great variety of trees and plants grows in the Amazon region.
12. Here, in this equatorial region, the chief mode of travel is by boat along the Amazon River.

_____
_____
_____
_____
_____
_____

© Steck-Vaughn Company

Critical Thinking 5, SV 6216-4

Name _____ Date _____

Abstract or Concrete

Groups of words that name related objects can be ranked from **abstract** to **concrete**. Usually a word that names a **particular** person or object is most **concrete**. Words become more abstract as they name categories that include more and more objects or people.

A. In each sentence below, there are four words or word groups that are related. Study the sentence and underline these related words or word groups. Then write **1** over the word or word group that is most abstract. Use the numerals **2**, **3**, and **4** over the other words as you narrow them down to the most concrete. The first sentence has been done for you.

1. <u>Mrs. Smith</u> (4) was voted the best <u>teacher</u> (3) of all <u>personnel</u> (2) working in our <u>school system</u> (1).

2. Henry Aaron was one of the best home-run hitters of all the batters who have been major league baseball players.

3. Dogs are among our favorite household pets, and the golden retriever is perhaps the favorite kind of hunting dog.

4. Among the trees chosen for yards, the maple is one of the most popular, and the red maple is one of the most spectacular plants.

B. Rewrite each sentence below, replacing the underlined words with ones that are more concrete.

1. He went into the <u>room</u> and prepared a <u>meal</u>. _____
   _____

2. She got into the <u>vehicle</u> and headed for the <u>roadway</u>. _____
   _____

3. We put the <u>liquid</u> into a <u>container</u>. _____
   _____

Name _____ Date _____

Logic of Actions

Actions are **logical** if they **make sense** in helping you to achieve a specific goal.

A. Suppose that you are the oldest of three children. Your sister is six and your brother is four. Your parents have asked that the three of you do the following chores before they return home from work. Write **sister**, **brother**, or **myself** after each chore to show the logical person you would assign to each job.

1. pick up toys _____
2. rake leaves _____
3. walk the dog _____
4. feed the cat _____
5. carry out the garbage _____
6. take the grocery list and go to the store _____
7. vacuum the living room rug _____
8. renew some books from the library _____
9. get the mail from the mailbox _____
10. polish the children's shoes _____

B. Suppose that it is holiday time. You have saved $16 with which to buy gifts for the following people: your parents, a younger brother or sister, a grandparent, your best friend. On the lines below, list in order at least five logical steps you would take before and during your shopping trip.

1. _____
2. _____
3. _____
4. _____
5. _____

Name _____ Date _____

Logic of Actions

A. Parking places were difficult to find, even in 1926. In that year, someone invented a lightweight car which had a set of small wheels at the back. To park the car, a person stood it up on these wheels. Was this a logical solution to the parking problem?

_____

Why or why not? _____

_____

Could we use this kind of solution for today's parking problems? _____

Why or why not? _____

_____

_____

B. Two classes were planning a trip. They found three possible places to go. Their problem was that the classes could not choose which one they liked best. Finally, Rosa suggested that the teachers break the deadlock by choosing a different place from the three the students had suggested.

Was this a logical plan? _____

Why or why not? _____

_____

On the lines below, write a logical suggestion of your own to solve the classes' problem.

_____

_____

_____

_____

58 © Steck-Vaughn Company   Critical Thinking 5, SV 6216-4

Name _____   Date _____

Elements of a Selection

Read this selection from *The Adventures of Tom Sawyer*. Then answer the questions that follow.

Tom appeared on the sidewalk with a bucket of whitewash and a long-handled brush. He surveyed the fence, and all gladness left him and a deep melancholy settled down upon his spirit. Thirty yards of board fence nine feet high. Life to him seemed hollow. . . .

He took up his brush and went tranquilly to work. Ben Rogers hove in sight presently—the very boy, of all boys, whose ridicule he had been dreading. . . .

"Hello, old chap, you got to work, hey?"

Tom wheeled suddenly and said: "Why, it's you, Ben! I warn't noticing."

"*Say*—I'm going in a-swimming. *I* am. Don't you wish you could? But of course you'd druther *work*—wouldn't you? Course you would!"

Tom contemplated the boy a bit, and said: "What do you call work?"

"Why, ain't *that* work?"

Tom resumed his whitewashing, and answered carelessly: "Well, maybe it is, and maybe it ain't. All I know is, it suits Tom Sawyer."

"Oh come, now, you don't mean to let on that you *like* it?"

The brush continued to move.

"Like it? Well, I don't see why I oughtn't to like it. Does a boy get a chance to whitewash a fence every day?"

That put the thing in a new light. Ben stopped nibbling his apple. . . . Presently he said: "Say, Tom, let *me* whitewash a little."

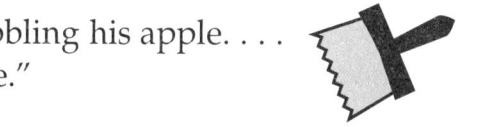

1. What kind of boy do think each character is?

   _____
   _____

2. What do you think will happen next in the plot?

   _____
   _____

3. Why do you think the author had the boys say words like *ain't* and *druther*?

   _____
   _____

Name _____ Date _____

Story Logic

A story is **logical** if it is told in an order that makes sense. Usually this order relates to time. The author begins with what happened first and ends with what happened last.

A. The outline below is not written in the correct time sequence. Rewrite the outline on the blank lines so that the sequence is correct.

Charles Dodgson

    II. Later life
- A. Wrote *Alice in Wonderland*
- B. Died in 1898
- C. Took the pen name Lewis Carroll

    I. Early life
- A. Teacher of mathematics
- B. Born in 1832

Charles Dodgson _____

    I. Early Life _____

_____

_____

_____

_____

_____

_____

B. Use your rewritten outline to write a short paragraph about the life of Charles Dodgson. Keep the facts in the correct sequence.

_____

_____

_____

_____

_____

Name _____ Date _____

Story Logic

Seven sentence parts are listed in the box. Decide where each sentence part fits logically within the article, and write it in the blank.

1. act as cleanup squads for debris
2. two pairs of wings
3. three fourths of all animal life
4. climate and food supply
5. three body segments
6. outer skeletons
7. provide food

An insect is an animal with an outside skeleton, a shell-like covering, and usually _____. An adult insect has six legs, and its appendages have joints. Insects have _____. These are the head, thorax, and abdomen.

Our world is teeming with insects. Insects comprise about _____ on our planet. Though most insects are tiny and live less than a year, they have not become extinct for several reasons. They have adapted to changes in _____; they are able to reproduce quickly; their bodies are protected by _____; and they are able to escape danger by flying.

While many kinds of insects are harmful, other kinds are useful. Insects _____ for birds, fish, and other small animals. Insects also pollinate plants and _____.

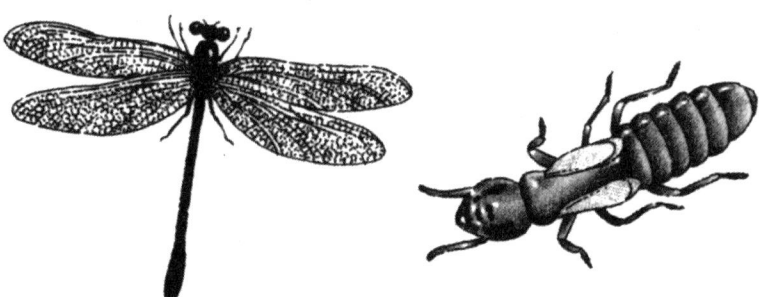

Dragonfly   **Termite**    **Butterfly**

© Steck-Vaughn Company   Critical Thinking 5, SV 6216-4   **61**

Name _____ Date _____

Recognizing Fallacies

A true **analogy** is a statement which shows the relationship between two pairs of words. The first pair of words shows what the relationship is about. Here are some examples:

- **Up** is to **down** as **over** is to **under**. (Relationship: opposites)
- **Second** is to **minute** as **hour** is to **day**. (Relationship: part of)
- **Clock** is to **time** as **scale** is to **weight**. (Relationship: function)

A. Write **opposite, part of,** or **function** after each analogy.

1. **Ounce** is to **pound** as **inch** is to **foot**. _____

2. **Saw** is to **cut** as **shovel** is to **dig**. _____

3. **In** is to **out** as **beautiful** is to **ugly**. _____

B. Make each analogy true by choosing the correct word to complete it.

1. **Rug** is to **floor** as **blanket** is to _____.
   warm   bed   wool

2. **Needle** is to **sew** as **hammer** is to _____.
   metal   tool   hit

3. **Shy** is to **bold** as **quiet** is to _____.
   loud   silent   sleep

C. The analogies below are false, because the last word in each one is incorrect. That is, the last word does not continue to show the relationship set up in the first pair of words. Cross out the last word. On the line, write the word that will make the analogy true.

1. **Scissors** are to **cut** as **rulers** are to **color**. _____

2. **Foot** is to **leg** as **hand** is to **body**. _____

3. **Happy** is to **sad** as **fast** is to **quick**. _____

4. **Pencil** is to **writing** as **brush** is to **comb**. _____

5. **Car** is to **drive** as **airplane** is to **wing**. _____

62   © Steck-Vaughn Company   Critical Thinking 5, SV 6216-4

Name _____ Date _____

Recognizing Fallacies

An **assumption** is an idea we reach before we have all the facts. Some assumptions turn out to be true. Others, however, turn out to be false. When all the facts are gathered, the assumption may prove to be wrong.

Read each item below. On line **1** make an assumption about the situation. On line **2** write why the assumption may be wrong.

A. A man climbs up a fire escape and opens a window to an apartment.

1. _____
2. _____

B. Amy plays the tuba. She decides to try out for the school band. On the day of tryouts, Amy sees a long line of students waiting by the band room. Amy goes home.

1. _____
2. _____

C. Dan grabbed the lunch bag and hurried to the cafeteria. As he began to eat, Clark came over. "That's my lunch," said Clark. "My name is written on the bottom of the bag." Clark turned the bag over. There was the name **Clark**.

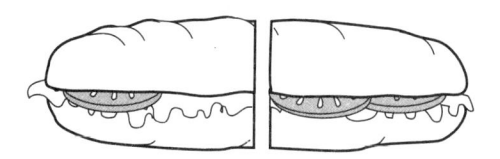

1. _____
2. _____

D. Sara was not doing well at school. She daydreamed in class. She seldom completed her homework. She was not willing to participate in class activities. When called on, her answers were usually wrong.

1. _____
2. _____

© Steck-Vaughn Company

Critical Thinking 5, SV 6216-4

Name _____   Date _____

Unit 4 Assessment Test

A. Elements of a Selection

Read the poem. Then do the activities that follow it.

The Bird of Night

A shadow is floating through the moonlight.
Its wings don't make a sound.
Its claws are long, its beak is bright.
Its eyes try all the corners of the night.

It calls and calls: all the air swells and heaves
And washes up and down like water.
The ear that listens to the owl believes
In death. The bat beneath the eaves,

The mouse beside the stone are still as death —
The owl's air washes them like water.
The owl goes back and forth inside the night,
And the night holds its breath.
—Randall Jarrell

1. What is the **setting** described in the poem?
   _____
   _____
   _____

2. Name the main character in the poem.
   _____
   _____
   _____

3. Is the main character real or fanciful?
   _____
   _____

B. Judging Completeness

List three phrases from the poem that help make the description of the owl complete.

1. _____
   _____

2. _____
   _____

3. _____
   _____

C. Logic of Actions

Why is it **logical** that the bat and the mouse stay very still as the owl flies by?

64   © Steck-Vaughn Company   Critical Thinking 5, SV 6216-4

Name _____ Date _____

Unit 4 Assessment Test (p. 2)

D. Recognizing Fallacies
Story Logic
Abstract or Concrete
Relevance of Information

Read the person's words. Then follow the directions that tell you how to rewrite the person's statement.

1. Rewrite the statement so that it is not an **either-or** fallacy.

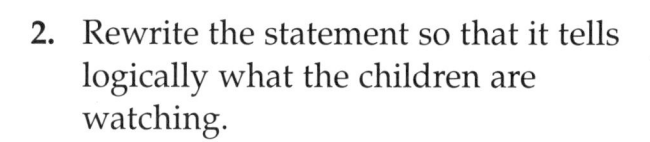

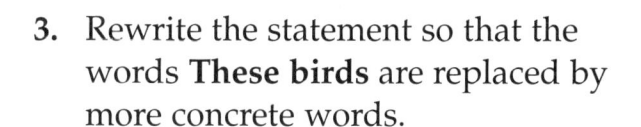

   _____

   _____

2. Rewrite the statement so that it tells logically what the children are watching.

   _____

   _____

3. Rewrite the statement so that the words **These birds** are replaced by more concrete words.

   _____

   _____

4. Rewrite the statement so that it tells where to find relevant information about myna birds.

   _____

   _____

© Steck-Vaughn Company

Critical Thinking 5, SV 6216-4

Name _____ Date _____

Unit 5 Synthesis
Communicating Ideas

A **concept** is a general idea we have about an object or a process. For example, the concept we have about **written information** is that it will be presented to us in fully spelled-out words and complete sentences. Sometimes, however, written information is presented in an **abbreviated** form. In such cases, you have to adjust your thinking so that you can understand the message.

In the following classified advertisements from a newspaper, the information is abbreviated. Study each advertisement. Then rewrite it in sentence form with the words fully spelled out.

1. FURNITURE SALE—Auto washer, 2 dr refrig, b & w TV, 4 pc BR set, 5 pc din set, misc lamps. E-Z terms.

2. NEED EXEC SECY—typ 70 wpm, shthnd, fil. Local ofc of nat'l co. Paid hosp ins, 2 wk vac, top hrly pay. 40 hr wk. Apply 8-5, M-F.

Name _____   Date _____

Communicating Ideas

A map can give you a fast visual idea of how water and land are related in space. Below is a map of the state of South Dakota, which is located in the northern part of the United States. Study the map. Notice where smaller rivers join to form larger rivers with new names.

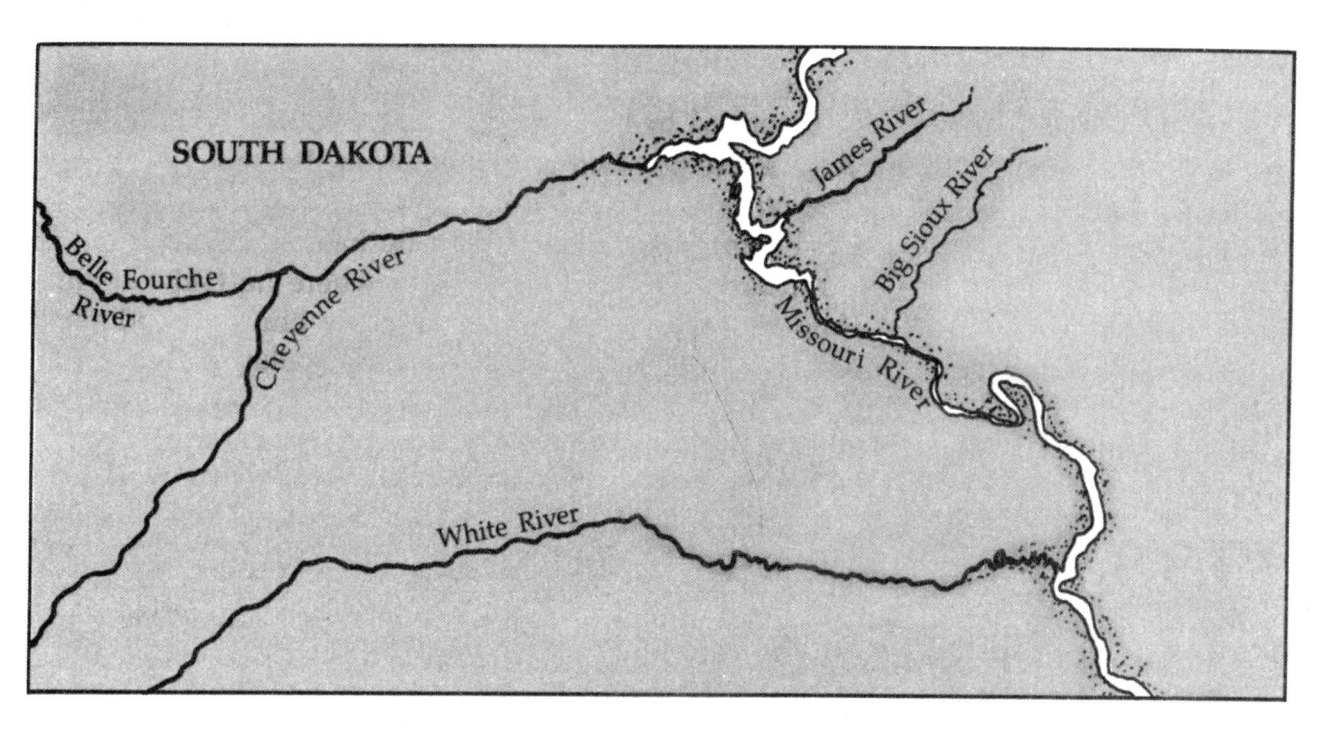

[Map of South Dakota showing Belle Fourche River, Cheyenne River, White River, James River, Big Sioux River, and Missouri River]

A. On the lines below, write a paragraph that describes the river system shown in the map.

_____

_____

_____

B. Which type of communication—the map or the paragraph—makes it easier to understand the river system? _____

Tell why you think so. _____

_____

_____

© Steck-Vaughn Company   Critical Thinking 5, SV 6216-4   **67**

Name _____ Date _____

Planning Projects

On Earth Day, members of the Science Club decided to clean the park across the street from their school. Below is an outline of their plan. Read each step to find out if their plan is complete. Add another idea to each step.

1. **Things to Do Before:**

    Get permission from principal.
    Get permission from park district.

    Other: _____
    _____

2. **Materials Needed:**

    Recyclable plastic bags to collect garbage

    Other: _____
    _____

3. **Steps to Follow:**

    Divide park into sections and assign groups of students to each section.

    Each group moves through its section, collecting garbage.

    Other: _____
    _____

4. **Time Needed:**

    Time to divide into groups = 5 minutes

    Time to pick up garbage = _____

    Other: _____
    _____

Name _____   Date _____

Planning Projects

A. Think about the following projects. Underline the one that you would prefer to carry out.

1. Show the effect of temperature and light on the growth of bean seeds.

2. Make a floor plan and model of the ideal school.

3. Identify ten birds common to your area by making drawings and recording the different birdcalls.

B. Complete the following lists to show how you would begin the project you selected in part A.

Supplies Needed

1. _____   4. _____

2. _____   5. _____

3. _____   6. _____

Five Major Steps to Take

1. _____

2. _____

3. _____

4. _____

5. _____

People to Consult or Ask for Help

1. _____

2. _____

Name _____ Date _____

Building Hypotheses

A **hypothesis** is a beginning explanation of what is happening or why something happened. A hypothesis may change as new facts are gathered.

The true story below is given in three parts. Read each part and answer the question that follows it. Then continue reading the story.

1. In the summer of 1890, millionaire Harry Lehr invited his friends to a dinner party. His friends were excited because he told them that a very special guest would be there. Mr. Lehr's wealthy friends were used to important people, but they were curious about the identity of this special guest.

    Who do you think the guest might be?

    _____

2. As the special guest entered, the other guests gasped in surprise. It was the Prince del Drago! He was attired elegantly in a black suit and tie. During dinner, however, the Prince did not talk to anyone. Silently, he ate his dinner.

    Why do you think this special guest was silent?

    _____

3. When he finished eating, the Prince left the table and jumped to the huge chandelier. Then he unscrewed the light bulbs and threw them crashing down onto the table.

    _____

    Circle the picture below that identifies the Prince del Drago. On the lines below the pictures, tell what facts in the story led you to this hypothesis.

    _____

Name _____ Date _____

Building Hypotheses

A. Five hypotheses and ten statements are listed below. Each hypothesis can be supported by facts. Which statements provide the facts that support each hypothesis? Write the letter of each statement before the hypothesis it supports. You will use more than one statement to support each hypothesis.

Hypothesis

_____ 1. Insecticides are not necessarily a sure way to kill mosquitoes.

_____ 2. The bathtub is one of the most dangerous areas in the home.

_____ 3. Some people dislike poetry.

_____ 4. Typewritten papers usually receive higher grades than handwritten papers.

_____ 5. Driver-training courses contribute to highway safety.

Statements

a. The hard material can cause broken bones and severe bruises.

b. Often it was not a part of their early learning.

c. They are easier to read.

d. Participants learn traffic laws and defensive driving attitudes.

e. There is proof that areas frequently sprayed still have many insects.

f. The enamel surface is so slippery that one can fall easily.

g. Driver-training graduates have fewer accidents than untrained drivers.

h. Some mosquitoes fly out of range of the spray.

i. Perhaps the subject was not presented in an interesting manner.

j. They have a more professional look.

B. Choose one of the hypotheses above. Write another statement to support it.

_____

Name _____   Date _____

Drawing Conclusions

A **conclusion** is a final statement you can make based on the facts given to you. Read the articles below. Make a check by each conclusion that could **not** be made from the facts given in the article.

A. Soil may be described as the earth's cover where the land stops and the air begins. Every ounce of fertile soil normally contains more living organisms than the human population of the entire world.

Soil provides a very effective sewage and waste disposal system. Earth's materials are recycled in the soil as life goes through generation after generation. It is unfortunate that much soil has been damaged through misuse, erosion, and the use of harmful chemicals.

_____ 1. Even poor soil is full of living things.

_____ 2. Good soil contributes to the cycle of life on Earth.

_____ 3. The earth's surface is covered with soil.

_____ 4. People have deliberately damaged the soil.

_____ 5. Scientists have carefully studied soil.

B. On May 25, 1961, U.S. President John Kennedy announced that the U.S. would land a person on the moon before the end of the decade. This tremendous mission cost $24 billion. The goal was finally reached when *Apollo 11* landed on the moon's surface on July 20, 1969. Neil Armstrong, Edwin Aldrin, and Michael Collins were on board *Apollo 11*. Armstrong and Aldrin spent 21 hours and 37 minutes on the moon before returning to the command ship.

_____ 1. Three astronauts walked on the moon.

_____ 2. The *Apollo* trip was costly.

_____ 3. President Kennedy was interested in the trip to the moon.

_____ 4. Several people wanted to go on the moon mission.

_____ 5. The astronauts faced incredible dangers.

Name _____ Date _____

Drawing Conclusions

If you understand someone's personality, you can often conclude what he or she will do in a certain situation. The pupils described below must take part in a class play. Read about each pupil. Then tell what particular task the pupil is likely to volunteer to do in the play.

1. Carla seems to have a special gift for working with color. Her friends always admire her paintings. She dresses in an original way. She has a knack for combining her clothes so that she always looks very special.

2. Mario is a great talker. He likes to tell jokes and is always ready to give colorful descriptions of things that have happened to him. Even from a distance, you can always identify Mario's voice, which rings with laughter.

3. Francine has a collection of notebooks in which she is always writing. One notebook is a journal about her personal experiences. Another notebook contains Francine's story ideas. In still another notebook, Francine lists interesting words she finds as she reads or as she listens to people talk.

4. When pupils are arguing over what game to play or what project to carry out, they very often call on Marta to settle the dispute. She has a way of solving problems and organizing activities that make her classmates like and respect her.

Carla's job in the play:

_____

Mario's job in the play:

_____

Francine's job in the play:

_____

Marta's job in the play:

_____

Name _____ Date _____

Drawing Conclusions

One day Samantha announced to her friends that she was a math wizard. "To prove this," said Samantha, "I want each of you to follow these steps:

1. Write a three-digit number in which the first and last digit differ by at least 2.
2. Reverse the digits in your number and write the new number.
3. You should now have two three-digit numbers. Subtract the smaller number from the larger one. Write down your answer.
4. Reverse the digits in your answer and write the new number.
5. Add this new number to your answer in step 3."

After Samantha's friends finished, Samantha whispered to each of them, "Your final answer is 1089." In each case, Samantha was absolutely right!

A. What is your conclusion about Samantha's magic trick?

_____

_____

B. On the lines below, test your conclusion by following steps 1 through 5 as given above.

_____

_____

_____

C. Check your conclusion again by asking a classmate or your teacher to carry out the steps.

D. Suppose your classmate or teacher comes up with an answer that is not 1089.

What will your conclusion be? _____

_____

74 © Steck-Vaughn Company   Critical Thinking 5, SV 6216-4

Name _____ Date _____

Proposing Alternatives

Study the situation described below. As you read, imagine that **you** are the baby-sitter.

One night, Leon accepted a job as baby-sitter for his neighbors' child Chrissy. The first part of the evening went well. Leon fed Chrissy her supper, read her a story, and tucked her into bed. After Chrissy fell asleep, Leon went downstairs to the kitchen and started to do his homework.

Suddenly, there was a howl from Chrissy's bedroom. Leon rushed upstairs. Chrissy was holding her stomach in pain. Tears were running down her cheeks. Leon felt Chrissy's forehead. It was as hot as a firecracker!

"Hold on, Chrissy!" said Leon. He ran downstairs again to look at the telephone message pad. Chrissy's parents had forgotten to leave important information! There was no doctor's number, no number that told where Chrissy's parents could be reached, and no numbers of neighbors or friends to call.

Chrissy was sick and needed help. Leon knew that!

What are three alternatives Leon could take in this situation?

1. _____

2. _____

3. _____

© Steck-Vaughn Company

Critical Thinking 5, SV 6216-4

75

Name _____ Date _____

Proposing Alternatives

Hula hoops were once extremely popular toys. The picture shows you how they were used. Although the hula game is out-of-date now, there might still be ways to use the leftover hoops.

A. Describe how you could use a hula hoop in each case below.

1. To teach someone how to tell time

   _____

   _____

2. For use in a relay race, where people run from one point to another

   _____

   _____

3. To show social studies data, such as population groups within a certain area

   _____

   _____

4. To teach someone about fractions

   _____

   _____

5. For use in an art project

   _____

   _____

B. On the lines below, describe another use of leftover hula hoops.

_____

_____

Name _____ Date _____

Unit 5 Assessment Test

**A. Communicating Ideas
Drawing Conclusions
Proposing Alternatives**

Study the material below. Then do the activities.

Caterpillar Thoughts

Shh! Don't bother me!
Leave me alone.
I'm busy as I can be,
Working my magic
In the dark

Inside this silk cocoon.
It's not easy
For a little worm
To grow such big, big
wings.

So shh! Don't bother me!
And see
What the springtime
brings.

Four Stages in the Life of a Butterfly

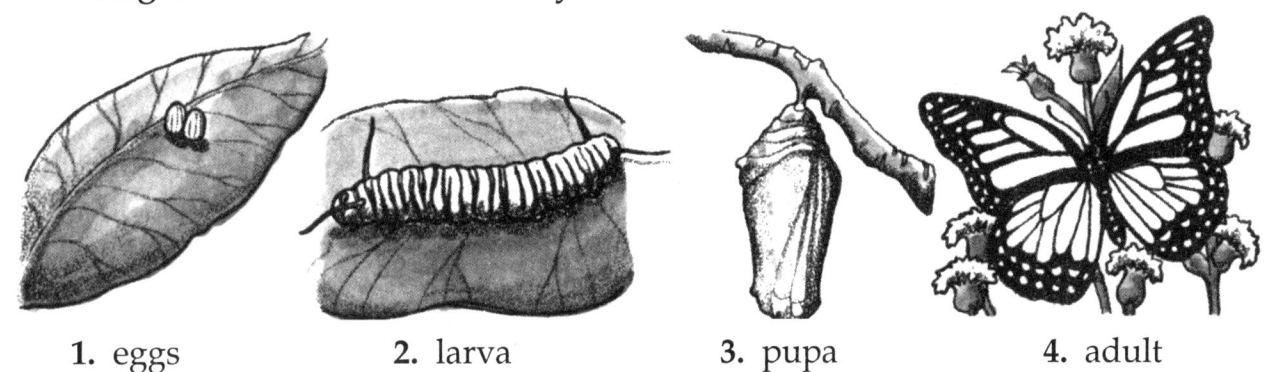

1. eggs   2. larva   3. pupa   4. adult

1. The materials above present the concept of **change**. In what two forms is the concept presented?

   _____

2. From the information given above, what insect stage do you conclude that the poet is telling about?

   _____

   What key words and phrases support your conclusion?

   _____

3. Propose an alternate way of telling about insect change. _____

   _____

© Steck-Vaughn Company   Critical Thinking 5, SV 6216-4   **77**

Name _____ Date _____

Unit 5 Assessment Test (p. 2)

B. Building Hypotheses

The pictures at the bottom of the page show four of the many kinds of animals that migrate.

1. Write a hypothesis telling what may cause some animals to migrate.

   _____
   _____

2. Name some of the sources you would consult to find out whether your hypothesis is correct.

   _____
   _____

C. Planning Projects

Imagine that you have been asked to join an oceanographic expedition to study the migration path of the humpback whale. Describe what specific job you would like to do in this project. Tell about materials and skills you would need.

_____
_____
_____
_____

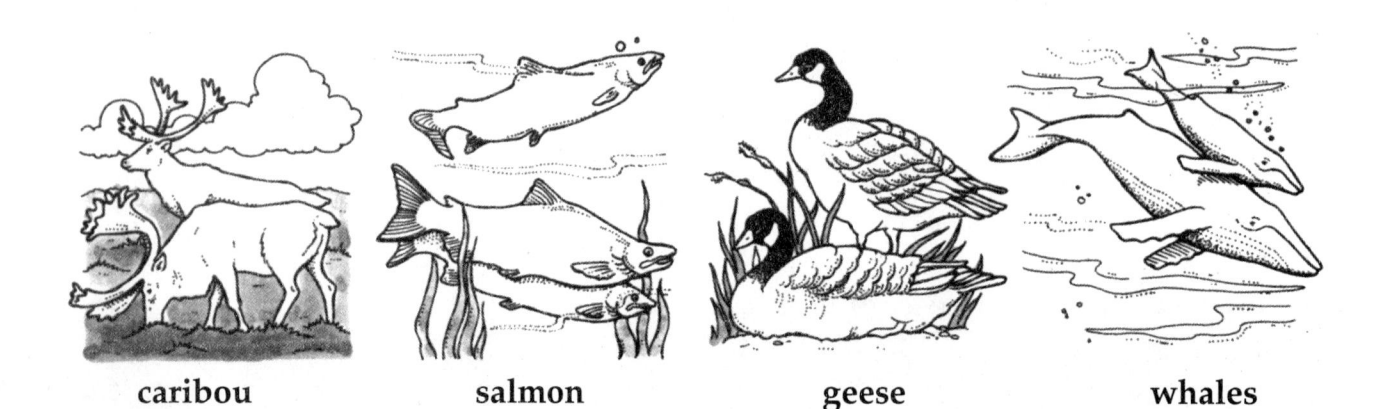

caribou   **salmon**   **geese**   **whales**

Name _____   Date _____

Unit 6 Evaluation
Testing Generalizations

Aesop's fables are stories that lead to generalizations about people's behavior—even though the characters in the fables are most often animals. Read each fable and choose the generalization from the box that fits the fable. Then explain whether the generalization is always true or whether in some real-life cases it is not.

> **Generalizations**
> The rich get richer, and the poor get poorer.
> Greed will only make you lose what you already have.
> Little by little does the trick.

A crow was half dead from thirst when it came upon a pitcher. Hopefully, it put its beak into the pitcher, but found only a little water left in the bottom. It tried and tried, yet it could not reach the water. Then a thought occurred to the crow. It took a pebble and dropped it into the pitcher. Then the crow took and dropped another pebble, and another, and another. Eventually, the water rose high enough, and the crow was able to drink.

_____
_____
_____

A dog was trotting home with a fine, meaty bone it had found, when it came upon a plank bridge crossing a stream. As the dog walked across the plank, it looked down and saw its reflection in the water. But the dog thought it was seeing another dog—one with an even larger and meatier bone. It made up its mind to have that bone, too. So it opened its mouth to snap the bone away from the other dog, dropping its own bone into the water and losing it forever.

_____
_____
_____

© Steck-Vaughn Company   Critical Thinking 5, SV 6216-4   **79**

Name _____ Date _____

Testing Generalizations

Read each paragraph. On the lines below it, write a true, or **valid**, generalization you can make from the facts given in the paragraph.

1. Imagine what would happen if all the glass around you should suddenly disappear! Insulated glass is used for windows, because it lets in light but keeps out hot and cold air. Glass is used in light bulbs, television tubes, mirrors, camera lenses, and eyeglasses. Even some cooking utensils and curtains are made of glass.

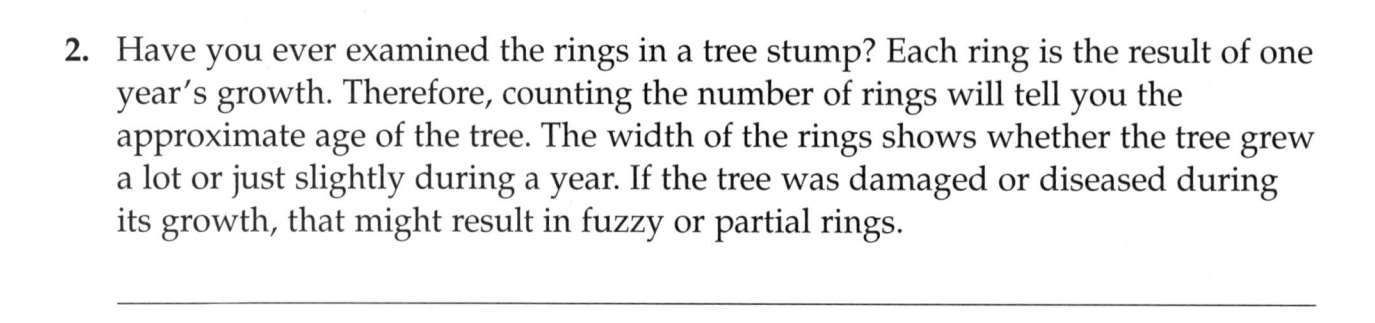

   _____
   _____
   _____

2. Have you ever examined the rings in a tree stump? Each ring is the result of one year's growth. Therefore, counting the number of rings will tell you the approximate age of the tree. The width of the rings shows whether the tree grew a lot or just slightly during a year. If the tree was damaged or diseased during its growth, that might result in fuzzy or partial rings.

   _____
   _____
   _____

3. Much of the land around the equator in Africa is densely forested wilderness. Tall trees spread their branches, shading the ground with heavy foliage. Near the ground, vines and creepers climb the trees and hang from limb to limb. The shady ground is covered with a thick growth of bushes with stems and branches so closely connected that it is difficult to clear a path without cutting the growth with each step.

   _____
   _____
   _____

© Steck-Vaughn Company

Critical Thinking 5, SV 6216-4

Name _____   Date _____

Developing Criteria

A **criterion** is a rule or guideline for judging or evaluating something. (The plural form of **criterion** is **criteria**.)

1. Suppose that your criterion for a tool is that it must measure time. Study the pictures below. Make an **X** on the tool or tools that do not meet that criterion.

   hourglass   digital watch   electric clock   measuring cup   cuckoo clock
                telescope   sundial   alarm clock

2. Expand your criteria. The timepiece must work without having to be wound, touched, or manipulated frequently. Write the names of the timepieces above which meet that criterion.

   _____
   _____
   _____

3. Change your criteria. The timepiece must make an obvious sound. Which timepieces above fill that criterion?

   _____
   _____

4. Imagine that you have been asked to design a wholly new kind of timepiece. You can make up your own criteria. What will they be?

   _____
   _____
   _____
   _____

© Steck-Vaughn Company   Critical Thinking 5, SV 6216-4

Name _____ Date _____

Developing Criteria

As you read, you often come across words that are unfamiliar to you. As a criterion for figuring out a word's meaning, you can use the context—or sentence—in which the word is used. As new details are provided in the sentence, your idea about the word's meaning can change.

Read sentence **1**. Use only the information in sentence 1 to fill in the blanks in the sentence below it. Next, read sentence **2**. Use the information provided in sentence 2 to fill in the sentence below it. Continue in this manner for all the sentences on this page.

| scarf | mosaic glass | wooden block |

1. Betsy was given a **tessera**.

   A **tessera** could be a _____, a _____, or a _____.

2. Betsy was given a **tessera** that had a hard surface.

   A **tessera** could be a _____ or a _____.

3. The **tessera** had a hard surface that reflected light.

   A **tessera** is a _____.

| lion | garment | bird |

4. Did you see the **ouzel**?

   An **ouzel** could be a _____, a _____, or a _____.

5. Did you see the **ouzel** eating its meal?

   An **ouzel** could be a _____ or a _____.

6. Did you see the **ouzel** eating seeds and berries?

   An **ouzel** is a _____.

© Steck-Vaughn Company

Critical Thinking 5, SV 6216-4

Name _____   Date _____

Judging Accuracy

When you read or listen, evaluate the accuracy of what the writer or speaker is saying. For example, listen or read to make sure there are no **contradictions**. In a contradiction, a person says one thing, and then later on says something that is just the opposite.

Read the following selections. Find and underline the sentences in each that contradict one another.

1. You can learn a lot by raising a young animal that you have found in the wild, such as a red squirrel or a raccoon. If you find a wild animal that is hurt or sick, call your local Humane Society. The people there will urge you to return the animal to its natural environment. When you raise a wild pet in your home, the Humane Society will gladly help you out.

2. In every state in the United States, it is a law that children must attend school until a certain age. Unless you attend school until that age, you or your parents could be taken to court. The law allows that "school" can mean being taught at home by your parents or going to a private school. In Mississippi, there is no law about attending school.

3. Most Americans respect George Washington, our first President, and have a special regard for his honesty. When Washington was only six years old, he admitted to his father that he had cut down a prized cherry tree. There is little doubt that Washington valued honesty and loyalty in government. The story about the cherry tree was made up by a man named Parson Weems, who sold 50,000 copies of his book about George Washington's life.

4. Children who run away from home often feel that they have very good reasons for doing so. Home may be a place where there is a lot of trouble and fighting, and it's best to stay away. Home is still the place where you can get the best help. Runaway children can get back home by calling one of the many "hotlines" for runaways.

© Steck-Vaughn Company

Critical Thinking 5, SV 6216-4 **83**

Name _____ Date _____

Judging Accuracy

When you are reading or listening, check to make sure that the conclusion follows logically from the facts that are given. If the conclusion does that, then it is accurate.

Study the picture and words below. Then do the activities.

> This is a great town. This is a great year. All of you are wonderful people. So, in conclusion, I can only say, "Vote for me!"

> What does he mean ... **in conclusion**?

> I didn't hear any facts leading up to **that** conclusion!

A. What is the speaker's conclusion? _____
_____

B. Why are the two young people in the audience doubtful about the conclusion?
_____
_____

C. Imagine that you are the speaker's speech writer. List three possible facts that the speaker could use to justify the conclusion, "Vote for me!"

1. _____
2. _____
3. _____

© Steck-Vaughn Company   Critical Thinking 5, SV 6216-4

Name _____ Date _____

Making Decisions

On many occasions, you are expected to provide **evidence** to prove that what you are saying is correct. Read about each situation described below. On the lines, write the kind of evidence you would expect each speaker to present.

1. One evening, a police officer stopped a driver who was moving along through traffic without using headlights. "I'm sorry, Officer," said the driver. "My headlights don't work. I just called the garage and was going there now to get the lights repaired."

   _____
   _____

2. The historical committee in a town asks that construction of a new housing project be stopped. "The site of the project," said the committee chief, "is an ancient Indian burial ground. It contains many valuable artifacts and should be preserved as a special forever-wild area."

   _____
   _____

3. The manufacturer of a new kind of glass claims that the product should be used for windows. A spokesperson for the company said, "The glass is unbreakable, conserves energy by keeping warm air from escaping, and lets in more light than other kinds of glass."

   _____
   _____

4. You announce after lunch that you found a valuable ring on the playground. "Hey, that's my ring," says one of your classmates. "I'm glad you found it. Please give it to me."

   _____
   _____

© Steck-Vaughn Company

Critical Thinking 5, SV 6216-4

85

Name _____ Date _____

Making Decisions

In preparing a report, you are usually expected to use resource material to find facts about your subject and to check those facts. Read each subject below. Then look at the book titles in the picture at the below. Write the titles of the books that you could consult for evidence.

Books on shelf: Encyclopedia, Vol. 8, M-N; The History of Transportation; Webster's College Dictionary; Florence Nightingale; Rand-McNally World Atlas; Travels in the South Pacific; Careers for YOU; The Encyclopedia of Natural History; Field Guide to Insects; Words and Their Meanings

1. a report on local moths and butterflies
   _____
   _____

2. a report on the rain forests of New Guinea
   _____
   _____

3. a report on nursing as a career
   _____
   _____

4. a report on English words from other languages
   _____
   _____

5. a report on the development of the highway system
   _____
   _____

86 © Steck-Vaughn Company

Critical Thinking 5, SV 6216-4

Name _____ Date _____

Making Decisions

The best decisions are made when you develop criteria for testing your decision. For example, when you decide whom to vote for as class president, you make your decision based on criteria.

1. Below are qualities some people have. The list was developed as criteria for choosing a class president. Decide how important you think it is for a president to have each quality. Rank the criteria from 1 to 10 in order of importance.

   _____ is popular with classmates

   _____ is able to lead people

   _____ is a very organized person

   _____ is a good student

   _____ has definite ideas about things to change around school

   _____ agrees with you on every issue

   _____ is attractive

   _____ gets along with the teacher

   _____ is a hard worker

   _____ is considerate of other people

2. Read the descriptions of two students who are running for class president. Decide whom you would vote for, based on your ranking of the criteria above. Place an **X** in the box next to that student's description. On the lines following the description, tell why you voted as you did.

☐ Maria Sanchez is the top student in class. She gets along well with people, but is not the most popular girl in school. Maria is a hard worker and very well organized. She wants to reorganize part of the school day so that students can spend a few minutes each day doing something for the community—food drives, recycling, and so on. She promises to listen to her classmates' ideas.

_____

☐ Paul Maki is a good student, but he is not the smartest person in class. He is very popular both with students and with teachers. Paul is tolerant and considerate of all people, and classmates seem to look up to him as a leader. He thinks everything around school is just fine, but he promises he would work hard if he found something that needed changing.

_____

© Steck-Vaughn Company

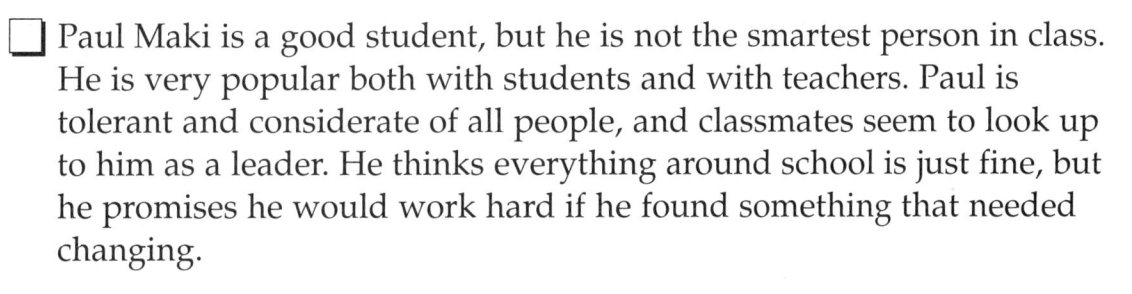

Critical Thinking 5, SV 6216-4

Name _____ Date _____

Identifying Values

The values that many people hold today were set down long ago in sayings and proverbs.

A. Read each old saying. Use your own words to tell what the saying means.

1. He who hesitates is lost.
   _____
   _____

2. Better late than never.
   _____
   _____

3. Haste makes waste.
   _____
   _____

4. Slow and steady wins the race.
   _____
   _____

5. Don't put off until tomorrow what you can do today.
   _____
   _____

B. Read the sayings—and your versions of them—carefully. Do you find that any of the values stated are in conflict? _____ Explain your answer on the lines below.

_____
_____

88 © Steck-Vaughn Company   Critical Thinking 5, SV 6216-4

Name _____   Date _____

Identifying Values

It often happens that a person's **own** values conflict with one another. Read about each person and situation. On the lines, tell **what** you think that person should do, and why you think he or she should do it.

1. Joel sets a high value on being kind to newcomers. He also sets a high value on playing fair and being a good sport.

    Kirk is a newcomer to school, and Joel, the captain of the kickball team, asks Kirk to join the team. During the very first game, Joel and his teammates notice that Kirk is a poor sport and often cheats. What should Joel, as captain, do?

    _____
    _____
    _____

2. Leon values honesty. He also values doing a good job on his schoolwork. He has been doing poorly in social studies, even though he has spent a lot of time studying.

    Tomorrow is the day of an important social studies test. Leon's friend Gary says, " I saw the teacher put the duplicated copies of the test in her desk drawer, and I'm going to take a copy at recess. Do you want me to get a copy for you, too?" What do you think Leon will do? Why?

    _____
    _____
    _____

3. Allison puts a high value on keeping her promises. She also puts a high value on friendship. Allison promised her little brother that she would take him to the park on Saturday. That morning Allison's friend Cindy calls and says, "Please come over. I feel so blue and need to talk to you alone." What do you think Allison should do? Why?

    _____
    _____
    _____

© Steck-Vaughn Company

Critical Thinking 5, SV 6216-4

Name _____ Date _____

Identifying Values

Imagine that it is the year 3000. All Earth people must choose a new planet on which to live. Their choices are the planets Alpha, Beta, or Gamma. Read the descriptions of each planet.

Alpha People do not do physical labor. It is done by machines. Children are raised in nurseries. When they become adults, people work in computer centers or at television broadcasting facilities dedicated to entertainment.

Beta Children are raised at home. Everyone must either attend school or work. All Beta people live exactly the same kind of life. Special awards and prizes, however, are given to citizens who perform special acts for their planet.

Gamma Gamma is known as the old-fashioned planet. Each family has a farm and is expected to provide everything for itself, from food to clothing and housing. There are no schools on Gamma. Children learn their parents' tasks and carry on the work of the farm when they grow up.

A. None of these three planets may suit you exactly. But suppose that you must choose one of them as your new home. Which planet would you choose?

_____

Why? _____

_____

B. Name three changes you would like to bring about on the planet you chose.

1. _____
2. _____
3. _____

© Steck-Vaughn Company

Critical Thinking 5, SV 6216-4

Name _____   Date _____

Mood of a Story

A writer builds a **mood**, or feeling, into a story in several ways. One of these ways is to appeal to values and emotions that many of us share. Read the story below. Then complete the activities.

> ### Waiting
>
> Hachi went to a Tokyo railroad station to see his master off to work as usual one day in 1925. At five o'clock, the faithful dog went to meet his master's homecoming train. But that night, his master did not appear and never would again, for he had died during the day.
>
> How was the loyal little dog to know that? Never giving up hope, Hachi went to the railroad station every day for the next ten years and waited for the five o'clock train. When his master did not appear, the dog slunk sadly home again.
>
> The story of the persistent dog spread throughout Japan, and the people came to love this special canine. When Hachi died, the Japanese government built a statue of the dog on the very spot where he had always waited. Tiny replicas of the statue were sent to all the schools in the nation.

1. In the story, find and underline the words or phrases that appeal to values of **affection**, **loyalty**, and **hope**.

2. Circle the phrase that sets a mood of despair or unhappiness.

3. Stories about dogs appeal to many people. On the lines below, list some reasons why this may be so.

   _____

   _____

4. Suppose that you are about to write a story or brief description of a dog. What mood would you try to establish?

   _____

   What words or phrases could you use to establish that mood?

Name _____ Date _____

Mood of a Story

Writers also establish story mood by carefully constructing descriptions of characters and by giving these characters dialogue that shows the characters in action.

Read each paragraph below. On the line before each paragraph, write a word from the box that best describes the character's mood or personality.

curious	ashamed	worried	grateful	kindhearted	angry

_____ 1. Vern pounded his fist on the table as he yelled at his brother. "How many times have I told you not to touch my experiment? You've ruined it! Now I'll have to start all over again," said Vern.

_____ 2. Sadie hang her head. "How could I have been so careless? Now none of you can go to the play, because I forgot to get the tickets. I'm so sorry," she said.

_____ 3. Owen walked to the window again and looked out at the storm. "I still don't see anyone coming down the road. The storm is getting worse. I hope they can get home safely," he said.

_____ 4. Ellen noticed a young boy sitting alone at the edge of the playground. She went over to him and suggested, "Come and join us. We're going to play dodge ball. If that isn't your favorite, we can play another game later."

_____ 5. Jesse purposely chose a seat in the cafeteria beside the new student. Before he even put his tray down, Jesse asked eagerly, "I hear you went to school in South America. What was it like? Which sports did you play?"

Name _____ Date _____

Unit 6 Assessment Test

A. Judging Accuracy
Making Decisions

This picture appeared in many newspapers all around the world in 1934. Study the picture for clues that will help you answer the questions below.

1. How can you tell that this is a birthday party?

   _____
   _____
   _____

2. In what way do these five girls seem special?

   _____
   _____
   _____

3. Suppose you are asked to find evidence to support your answer to question 2. What source could you use?

   _____
   _____
   _____

B. Testing Generalizations

Study the following generalization. Then rewrite it to make it valid.

All children who are special get a lot of publicity and extra attention.

_____
_____

© Steck-Vaughn Company   Critical Thinking 5, SV 6216-4

93

Name _____ Date _____

Unit 6 Assessment Test (p. 2)

C. Mood of a Story

Read the poem. Then complete the activities that follow it.

Mama Is a Sunrise

When she comes slip-footing through the door,
    she kindles us
    like lump coal lighted,
    and we wake up glowing.
She puts a spark even in Papa's eyes
and turns out all our darkness.

When she comes sweet-talking in the room,
    she warms us
    like grits and gravy,
    and we rise up shining.
Even at night-time Mama is a sunrise
that promises tomorrow and tomorrow.

—Evelyn Tooley Hunt

1. Write a sentence that describes the mood of the poem.

   _____
   _____
   _____

2. On the lines below, develop two sets of criteria—one for the "perfect parent" and one for the "perfect child."

   Perfect Parent   **Perfect Child**

   _____   _____
   _____   _____
   _____   _____

© Steck-Vaughn Company   Critical Thinking 5, SV 6216-4

Answer Key

Page 6
A., B., C. Answers will vary.
Page 7
1. Answers will vary. 2. books about animals, encyclopedias, textbooks E. Answers will vary.
Page 9
1. C 2. E 3. E 4. A 5. D 6. B 7. A 8. F 9. A 10. B
Page 10
Immediate Family - brother, sister, mother, father, stepfather, stepmother: Male -cousin, brother, stepfather, grandfather, uncle, father: Same Generation as You - cousin, brother, sister: Other Relatives - aunt, cousin, grandmother, grandfather, uncle: Female - aunt, cousin, mother, grandmother, sister, stepmother: Older Generation than You - aunt, mother, stepfather, grandmother, grandfather, uncle, father, stepmother
Page 11
Stringed: cellos, violins, guitar Wind: piccolos, flutes, tubas, trumpet Percussion: bass drums, triangle, cymbals - percussion and stringed: percussion because the piano keys are struck, and stringed because piano strings are moved by hammers
Page 12
Realistic Story: Daniel sat at the school's new computer and turned it on. The computer whirred, buzzed, clicked, and then showed a prompt sign. Daniel inserted a disk and hit a few keys. He had a great idea for a story. Fantasy: Daniel sat at the school's new computer and turned it on. The computer whirred, buzzed, clicked, and then showed a prompt sign. Daniel thought he must be mistaken when he saw the keyboard typing by itself. Then Daniel saw this message on the screen: "Wait till you see what I can do!"
Page 13
1. several 2. made a swishing sound 3. fireflies 4. 105 5. near freezing 6. as high as a redwood tree 7. very beautiful 8. almost deafen us for the moment 9. very rapidly
Page 14
A. 1. Fact: John bought a new car Opinion: which he thinks is the best car ever made. 2. Opinion: Because she felt that she might get a lot of attention, Fact: Peg joined the basketball team. 3. Fact: Darren and Hank bravely walked into the forest Opinion: that everyone believed was haunted. 4. Opinion: "You surely have the most beautiful house in town," Fact: Lila said when she came to visit Judy. 5. Fact: When the class judged the pictures, Opinion: most of the students thought Art's drawing was the best.
B. 1. O 2. F 3. F 4. O 5. O
Page 15
1. fact 2. fact 3. opinion 4. opinion 5. fact 6. opinion 7. opinion 8. opinion 9. opinion 10. fact
Page 16
A. 2. J, G 3. B, E 4. D, F 5. H, A B. Answers will vary according to the dictionaries used.
Page 17
2. D, E, seat 3. E, plant, D 4. D, E, shelter 5. D, E, bird 6. D, E, tool 7. D, E, weather 8. E, emotion, D
Page 18
A. Answers will vary. Suggestion: Summary 2 gives the main idea of the entire paragraph. Summary 1 is an opinion. Summary 3 tells only about certain details of the paragraph.
B. Answers will vary, but each should be briefer than the paragraph above.

Page 19
Suggested Answers: I. A. Produces honey and helps flowers grow B. Symbolizes hard work II. A. Traps insects and sucks blood B. Symbolizes misers III. A. Moves slowly B. Symbolizes laziness IV. A. Changes its form B. Symbolizes the process of life
Page 20
A. 1. 17, 10, 19, 20, 16 2. 12, 1, 18, 14, 11, 15 3. 5, 7, 4, 3 4. 13, 9, 6, 2, 8
B. Main topics of outline should be: I. Stationery II. Writing Tools III. Decorations IV. Packaging; Details, lettered A., B., etc., should be drawn from the labels shown in the picture.
Page 21
C. 1. like diamonds, like marbles, blink like traffic lights 2. Paragraphs will vary.
D. Sentences will vary.
Page 22
A. 1. Answers will vary. Possible answers: a. They both have wings. b. They both have beaks. 2. a. They are different sizes. b. One is a water bird and the other is not.
B. Likenesses 1. Unusual nests 2. Chicks dig through barriers Differences 1. Nests made differently 2. Different incubation time
Page 23
Answers will vary.
Page 24
A. Structure II. Line 1: My hat Line 2: Fuzzy, warm, soft Line 3: Protects, covers, cuddles Line 4: Makes a whirl of color on snow Line 5: Ski cap B. Poems will vary in subject matter, but all should adhere to Structure I.
Page 25
A. 2. talk, speak 3. boat, ship 4. fury, rage 5. turn, spin 6. quit, leave B. 2. trust, rely 3. spot, stain 4. hate, ship 4. fury, rage 5. turn, spin 6. quit, leave B. 2. trust, rely 3. spot, stain 4. hate, detest 5. swap, trade 6. crave, desire 7. peal, ring 8. sleep, nap 9. fear, dread 10. steal, rob
Page 26
A. Answers will vary but should tell the story in sequence. B. 4, A police officer would not tell a cat about a traffic sign. C. fanciful, It would not really happen.
Page 27
Probable responses: 2. Force spouts into the holes. 3. Hang buckets from spouts to collect sap. 4. Pour sap into large tanks. 5. Take tanks to sap house. 6. Boil sap.
Page 28
A. Kim, Jean 2. Juan, 80 3. Sandy, Bob
B. 1. game 5 2. 20 3. 2, 4 4. George improved as he played.
Page 29
2. pen 3. wheel 4. ring 5. shell 6. star 7. teeth 8. story 9. plate 10. bed 11. glass 12. key 13. table 14. light 15. nail
Page 30
Game I: vertically - accentuate, expire, elect, hug, mislay, tumult, qualified, radiant, ragged Game II: vertically - rapid, reaction, ready, genuine, reap, revolt, restore, remember, sensational
Page 31
A. 1. no topic sentence 2. The camel is well-equipped for desert travel. 3. no topic sentence 4. Though insects are small, many of them can cause great damage. B. Answers will vary but should encapsulate the main idea.
Page 32
A. Draw a line through #3. Topic sentences will vary. B. Draw a line through #2. Topic sentences will vary.

Page 33
1. check, circle *when* 2. circle *after*, underline *parking the car.* 3. circle *before*, underline *Jim could tell that something strange was going on.* 4. check, circle *as* 5. underline *He was not frightened*, circle *until* 6. underline *He hesitated*, circle *then* 7. check, circle *while* 8. circle *after*, underline *deciding to look now or never* 9. check, circle *when* 10. underline *Looking puzzled, Jim stepped into the room*, circle *then* 11. check, circle *At the same moment* 12. circle *after*, underline *Jim's excitement was over*
Page 34
A. 1. Because or Since 2. As a result 3. Because or Since B. Answers will vary.
Page 35
Answers will vary. Possible responses: 1. Mrs. Brown sent the toy to Vivian. 2. Water flowed down the mountainside into the stream. 3. Jane wanted to help her parents get some money together. 4. Yuji and his friends save money through a car-pool. 5. The town's population decreased.
Page 36
Answers will vary.
Page 37
D. The sun and nine planets make up the solar system. The sun lies at the center. The planets travel around the sun in oval-shaped paths, or orbits. E. Except for Pluto, the farther planets are much larger than the closer planets.
F. Earth is the third planet from the sun. Venus lies between Earth and the sun. Sometimes Pluto moves between Neptune and the sun.
Page 38
A. Column 1: 4, 2, 1, 6, 3, 5 Column 2: 3, 6, 2, 4, 1, 5 Column 3: 3, 6, 1, 2, 4, 5 B. 1, 8, 5, 7, 2, 4, 3, 6
Page 39
2: 3, 2, 1 3: 2, 3, 1 B. 1: 2, 1, 3 2: 2, 1, 3 3: 3, 1, 2
C. Answers will vary. Examples are given. Standard 1: Size - roller skate, wheelbarrow, bicycle, tractor-trailer Standard 2: Number of Wheels - wheelbarrow, bicycle, roller skate, tractor-trailer
Page 40
A. 1. Answers will vary. 2. house, car or piano, car or piano, bed or television, bed or television, light bulb or bread 3. house - television, car, bed or piano - may be listed in varying orders - light bulb - bread B. Answers will vary.
Page 41
Accept any estimate that is within an acceptable range of the estimates given. New York: 200 mi (325 km), 1400 mi (2250 km), 875 mi (1400 km), 2850 mi (4600 km) Miami: 1500 mi (2400 km), 850 mi (1300 km), 1375 mi (2200 km) Los Angeles: 3300 mi (5300 km), 1900 mi (3100 km), 1800 mi (2900 km), 1125 mi (1800 km) Dallas: 1800 mi (2900 km), 450 mi (700 km), 900 mi (1450 km), 2000 mi (3200 km)
Page 42
Answers will vary.
Page 43
Answers will vary. Possibilities are given. 1. a water shortage will be declared. 2. will be a success. 3. the player will often get the ball through the hoop. 4. you will go hungry.
B. Answers will vary. Possibilities are given. 1. a. schedule some practice time together. b. do well in their duet. 2. a. overcome his fears and go on the trip. b. ask to stay with someone he knows.
Page 44
A. 1. probability 2. probability 3. possibility 4. possibility 5. possibility B. Answers will vary.

Answer Key (p. 2)

Page 45
Answers will vary.

Page 46
1. Answers will vary but should take the facts above into account. 2. Answers will vary. Possibilities: friendship, a source of income, help from neighbors to get his house in order. 3. Answers will vary. Possibilities: Ask Mr. M. Ask a social worker. Discuss the situation with neighbors.

Page 47
1, 3, 7, 8

Page 48
A. 3, 2, 1 B. Answers will vary according to which underlined word the pupil decides to replace.

Page 49
A. 1. run into 2. saw through 3. fell behind 4. looked on 5. takes after B. Answers will vary. Possibilities: 1. run into, meet 2. saw through, understood the falsity of 3. fell behind, failed to keep up 4. looked on, watched 5. takes after, resembles

Page 50
A. Labels and their placement will vary, but the total picture should show items organized in a logical way. Answers will vary. Possible responses are listed: unpack goods, clean store, hire workers, arrange items on shelves, price items B. Answers will vary. Possibilities: The Whites have enough money to make a big investment. The Whites are experienced storekeepers. The town needs a large department store.

Page 51
C. Answers will vary. Possibilities: Employees will be confused. (or) Employees may be upset. 2. Employees may feel that the Whites will be hard to please. D. Answers will vary but should be brief and complete.

Page 52
Answers will vary. Possibilities are given. 1. what kind of bicycle it is; the model number. 2. what size lawn mower is wanted; how much the customer is willing to spend; where the customer lives. 3. what grades will be participating; when the show will take place; what room or rooms will be used; who is to be invited to the show. 4. the subject of the composition; how long it should be; when the composition is due. 5. how old the child is; when the party will take place; where it will take place; how many guests there will be; what kind of food your parents want to have served.

Page 53
1. F 2. F 3. T 4. T 5. T 6. F 7. T 8. T 9. F

Page 54
1. recipe book, cookbook 2. health book, first-aid book 3. gardening book, instructions on a package of zinnia seeds 4. astronomy book, science book 5. spelling book, dictionary 6. individual books describing careers, counseling books 7. chart on cursive letters, handwriting book 8. hospital manual, book about careers 9. newspaper, recent science magazines

Page 55
Paragraphs will vary but should contain the facts given in the ten relevant sentences above. Sentences 9 and 10 are not relevant.

Page 56
2. Henry Aaron-4, home-run hitters-3, batters-2, major league baseball players-1 3. Dogs-2, household pets-1, golden retriever-4, hunting dog-3 4. trees-2, maple-3, red maple-4, plants-1 B. Answers will vary.

Page 57
Answers will vary.

Page 58
Answers will vary.

Page 59
Answers will vary. 1. Tom is clever. Ben makes fun of others and is easily fooled. 2. Tom will get Ben to whitewash the fence. 3. He wanted them to sound like boys from a particular area in the United States. He also wanted to show that the conversation taking place was informal.

Page 60
A. A. Born in 1832 B. Teacher of mathematics II. Later life A. Took the pen name Lewis Carroll B. Wrote *Alice in Wonderland* C. Died in 1898 B. Paragraphs will vary but should be sequential.

Page 61
two pairs of wings, three body segments, three fourths of all animal life, climate and food supply, outer skeletons, provide food, act as cleanup squads for debris

Page 62
A. 1. part of 2. function 3. opposite B. 1. bed 2. hit 3. loud C. 1. measure 2. arm 3. slow 4. painting 5. fly

Page 63
Answers will vary.

Page 64
A. 1. night in the woods 2. an owl 3. real B. Answers will vary. C. They do not want the owl to catch them.

Page 65
D. Answers will vary. Possibilities: 1. You probably will like some kinds of birds better than other kinds. 2. I think birds are fascinating. 3. Ostriches and penguins can't fly. 4. If you read a book about pet birds, you can find out how to teach a myna bird to talk.

Page 66
Answers will vary slightly Possibilities: 1. We are having a furniture sale. We are selling an automatic washer, a two-door refrigerator, a black-and-white TV set, a four-piece bedroom set, a five-piece dining room set, and miscellaneous lamps. We can offer you easy terms for payment. 2. I need an executive secretary who can type 70 words per minute, take shorthand, and file. The job is in the local office of a national company. The employee will get hospital insurance, a two-week vacation, and top hourly pay for a 40-hour week. Apply 8 a.m. to 5 p.m., Monday through Friday.

Page 67
A. Answers will vary. B. Probable answer: the map. Answers will vary but most will state that some concepts are easier to understand in visual form than in verbal form.

Page 68
Answers will vary. 1. Scout park to determine how much litter there is; find out where to put garbage bags. 2. ties to close bags; gloves to pick up messy garbage 3. Assign pupils to collect bags as they are filled and to distribute more garbage bags. 4. depends on amount of garbage and size of park - advance scouting required, Other: time to get to and from the park

Page 69
Answers will vary according to the project chosen by the pupil.

Page 70
1. Answers will vary. Example: It might be a famous actor or political figure. 2. He might be shy or he might not speak English. 3. Answers will vary. Examples: He could not talk. He caused other guests to gasp. He could jump onto the chandelier. He played a monkey-like trick.

Page 71
A. 1. e, h 2. a, f 3. b, i 4. c, j 5. d, g B. Answers will vary.

Page 72
A. 1, 3, 4, 5 B. 1, 4, 5

Page 73
Probable responses. Carla - She will design the costumes. Mario - He will be an actor or announcer. Francine - She will help write the play. Marta - She will be the director.

Page 74
A. The answer to this process is always 1089. D. The classmate or teacher has made a mistake in carrying out one of the steps.

Page 75
Answers will vary. Possibilities: 1. Call his parents. 2. Find the number of his own doctor, and ask that doctor for help. 3. Run next door and ask a neighbor to help him.

Page 76
Answers will vary.

Page 77
1. The concept is presented in poetry form and in picture form. 2. pupa Answers will vary. Examples: inside, cocoon, dark, working my magic, wings 3. Answers will vary.

Page 78
Answers will vary.

Page 79
Answers will vary. 1. Little by little does the trick; not always true. 2. Greed will only make you lose what you already have; not always true.

Page 80
Answers will vary.

Page 81
1. measuring cup and telescope 2. sundial, electric clock, digital watch 3. cuckoo clock, alarm clock 4. Answers will vary.

Page 82
1. scarf, mosaic glass, wooden block 2. mosaic glass, wooden block 3. mosaic glass 4. lion, garment, bird 5. lion, bird 6. bird

Page 83
1. The people there will urge you to return the animal to its natural environment. When you raise a wild pet in your home, the Humane Society will gladly help you out. 2. In every state in the United States, it is a law that children must attend school until a certain age. In Mississippi, there is no law about attending school. 3. When Washington was only six years old, he admitted to his father that he had cut down a prized cherry tree. The story about the cherry tree was made up by a man named Parson Weems, who sold 50,000 copies of his book about George Washington's life. 4. Home may be a place where there is a lot of trouble and fighting, and it's best to stay away. Home is still the place where you can get the best help.

Page 84
A. He concludes that people should vote for him. B. There are no facts to support it. C. Answers will vary but should deal with the speaker's background and experience.

Page 85
Answers will vary, but all should focus on the necessity to present facts and evidence.

Page 86
1. *Encyclopedia, Vol. 8, M-N; The Encyclopedia of Natural History; Field Guide to Insects* 2. *Rand-McNally World Atlas; Travels in the South Pacific* (also possible: *The Encyclopedia of Natural History*) 3. *Encyclopedia, Vol. 8, M-N; Careers for You* 4. *Webster's College Dictionary; Words and Their Meanings* 5. *The History of Transportation*

Page 87
Answers will vary.

Page 88
A. Answers will vary. B. Yes. Answers will vary but should point out that some of the sayings put a high value on proceeding slowly, and others put a high value on proceeding quickly.

Page 89
Answers will vary.

Page 90
Answers will vary.

Page 91
1. faithful, loyal little dog, Never giving up hope, the persistent dog, the very spot where he had always waited 2. the dog slunk sadly home again 3. Answers will vary. 4. Answers will vary.

Page 92
1. angry 2. ashamed 3. worried 4. kindhearted 5. curious

Page 93
A. 1. There are candles on the cake. 2. They are sisters; they look the same age; they are dressed alike. 3. Suggestions: Look in newspaper files for special events of 1934; ask a parent or grandparent if they know the children in the picture. B. Answers will vary but should mention that many children are special and do not get worldwide attention.

Page 94
Answers will vary.